TRAINS

CONSULTANT – MICHAEL HARRIS

HERMES
HOUSE

This edition is published by Hermes House

Hermes House is an imprint of Anness Publishing Ltd
Hermes House, 88–89 Blackfriars Road, London SE1 8HA
tel. 020 7401 2077; fax 020 7633 9499; info@anness.com

A CIP catalogue record for this book is available from
the British Library.

Publisher: Joanna Lorenz
Managing Editor, Children's Books: Gilly Cameron Cooper
Principal Text Contributor: Jackie Gaff
Project Editors: Jenni Davidson and Leon Gray
Copy Editor: Dawn Titmus
Designer: Caroline Reeves, Aztec Design
Photographer: John Freeman
Stylist: Melanie Williams
Picture Researcher: Gwen Campbell
Illustrator: Peter Bull Art Studio
Editorial Reader: Joy Wotton
Production Controller: Darren Price

The publishers would like to thank the following
children, and their parents, for modelling in this book:
Tyrone Agiton, Erin Bhogal, Stacie Damps, Brooke
Griffiths, Eddie Lengthorn, Nicky Payne,
Zoe Richardson and Ajvir Sandhu.

PICTURE CREDITS
b=bottom, t=top, c= centre, l= left, r= right

Alvey and Towers Picture Library: 22cl, 31tl, 41t, 41cl, 41br, 49c, 57br;
Colin Boocock: 25br; Corbis/Morton Beebe, S.F.: 57t; Corbis/Bettmann: 27cl;
Corbis/Dallas and John Heaton: 56b; Corbis/John Heseltine: 23bl; Corbis/Jeremy Horner:
34tl; Corbis/Hulton Getty: 40cl; Corbis/Wolfgang Kaehler: 49b; Corbis/Lake County
Museum: 5t; Corbis/Milepost 92½: 37tl; Corbis/Paul A. Souders: 25tl; Corbis/Michael S.
Yamashita: 27tr, 32b, 46tr; Chris Dixon: i, 58br; Mike Harris: iit, 57cr, 58bl; Anthony J.
Lambert Collection: front cover (br), 4t, 21tr, 23br, 48tl, 55tl; *The Illustrated London News:*
38t, 38br, 48bl; The Kobal Collection: 52bl, 52br, 52tl, 53tr, 53bl, 53br, 63bl;
London Underground Ltd: 15cr; Mary Evans Picture Library: 12b, 14t, 15t,
15cl, 16t, 16b, 20t, 20c, 22tl, 26tr, 26b, 36cr, 36bl, 40br; Milepost 92½:
front cover (tl, tr, cl, cr, bl), back cover (tl, tr, cl, cr), iib, iiicl, iiibl, 4c, 5cl,
5cr, 6t, 8b, 9bl, 9br, 10t, 13cl, 13cr, 17c, 17b, 18t, 20b, 21tl, 21cr, 21b,
22cr, 23t, 24t, 24b, 25tr, 25bl, 27b, 31tr, 33t, 33cr, 37cl, 37br, 39tl, 39cl,
42tr, 44bl, 44br, 45t, 45c, 45b, 48br, 50tr, 52tr, 57cl, 58t, 59tl, 62tr;
Millbrook House Ltd: 26c, 28tl; Brian Morrison: 13b, 63tr; QA Photos Ltd:
39cr; Claire Rae: 55cr; RAWIE: 33bl, 33bc; Science and Society/
National Railway Museum: iiitr, iiicr, 8t, 36t, 54b, 60t; Science and Society/
London Transport Museum: 40tl; SNCF-CAV/Sylvain Cambon: 15b;
SNCF-CAV/Jean-Marc Fabbro: 30b.

Every effort has been made to trace the copyright holders of all images that appear in this
book. Anness Publishing Ltd apologises for any unintentional omissions and, if notified,
would be happy to add an acknowledgement in future editions.

10 9 8 7 6 5 4 3 2 1

TRAINS

CONTENTS

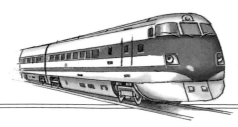

RUNNING ON RAILS

THROUGHOUT HISTORY, people have looked for ways to move themselves and their possessions faster and more efficiently. Wheels were invented about 5,500 years ago. As wheels are round, they turn well on smooth surfaces and reduce the rubbing, slowing force called friction. However, it soon became clear that wheels do not work well on rough, soft or muddy ground.

To solve this problem, tracks of wood or stone were cut into or laid onto the ground to provide a smooth surface on which wheels could turn. This kept friction to a minimum, so that vehicles could move more easily and shift heavier loads.

The ancient Greeks made the first railed tracks in about 400BC by cutting grooved rails into rock. They hauled ships overland by setting them on wheeled cars that ran along the tracks. Iron rails came into use in Europe by the mid-1700s. They were laid, mainly in mines, to transport cars loaded with coal or metal ores. Steam-powered locomotives were developed in the early 1800s. Before then, cars in mines were pulled by horses or by the miners themselves, which was slow and only possible for short distances.

Pulling power
A horse pulls a freight car along rails. Modern railroads developed from ones first laid in European mines in the mid-1500s. Heavy loads, such as coal and metal ore, were carried in cars with wheels that ran along wooden planks. The cars were guided by a peg under the car, which slotted into a gap between the planks. Horses and sometimes even human laborers were used to haul the cars long before steam locomotives were invented.

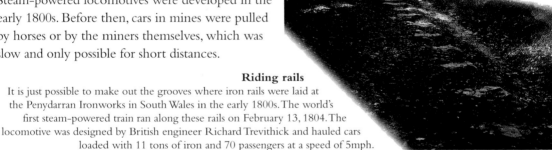

Riding rails
It is just possible to make out the grooves where iron rails were laid at the Penydarran Ironworks in South Wales in the early 1800s. The world's first steam-powered train ran along these rails on February 13, 1804. The locomotive was designed by British engineer Richard Trevithick and hauled cars loaded with 11 tons of iron and 70 passengers at a speed of 5mph.

1769–1810	1811–1830	1831–1860	1861–1880
1769 FRENCHMAN NICHOLAS CUGNOT builds the first steam-powered vehicle.	**1825** THE STOCKTON AND DARLINGTON RAILWAY opens in Britain—the first public railroad to use steam-powered locomotives.	**1833** GEORGE STEPHENSON devises the steam brake cylinder to operate brake blocks on the driving wheels of steam locomotives.	**1863** LONDON UNDERGROUND'S Metropolitan Line opens and is the world's first underground passenger railroad.
	1827 THE BALTIMORE AND OHIO RAILROAD is chartered to run from Baltimore to the River Ohio, Virginia, in the USA.		**1864** AMERICAN GEORGE PULLMAN builds the first sleeping car, the *Pioneer*.
1804 BRITISH ENGINEER RICHARD TREVITHICK tests the first steam locomotive for the Penydarran Ironworks in Wales.	**1829** ROBERT AND GEORGE STEPHENSON'S *Rocket* wins the Rainhill Trials. It becomes the locomotive used for the Liverpool and Manchester Railway.		**1868** PULLMAN builds the first dining car.
			1869 THE CENTRAL PACIFIC and Union Pacific railroads meet at Promontory Summit, linking the east and west coasts of the USA.
1808 TREVITHICK builds a circular railroad in London, Britain, and exhibits the *Catch Me Who Can* locomotive.		**1840s** SEMAPHORE SIGNALING is introduced. First tickets for train journeys are issued.	**1872** AMERICAN GEORGE WESTINGHOUSE patents an automatic air-braking system.

Trackless trains

The world's longest trackless train runs at Lake County Museum in Columbia, South Carolina, in the USA. Trackless trains are common in theme parks. They carry passengers in carts or wagons running on rubber-tired wheels. The trains are pulled by a tractor that is made to look like a railroad locomotive.

Puffing Billy

The locomotive in this painting was nicknamed *Puffing Billy* because it was one of the earliest to have a smokestack. It was designed by British mine engineer William Hedley and built in 1813. The first steam engines were built in the early 1700s. They were used to pump water from mineshafts, not to power vehicles. *Puffing Billy* can be seen today in the Science Museum in London, Britain. It is the world's oldest surviving steam locomotive.

Modern rail networks

Today, nearly all countries in the world have their own railroad network. Thousands of miles of track crisscross the continents. Steam power has now given way to newer inventions. Most modern trains are hauled by locomotives powered by diesel engines, by electricity drawn from overhead cables, or from an electrified third rail on the track.

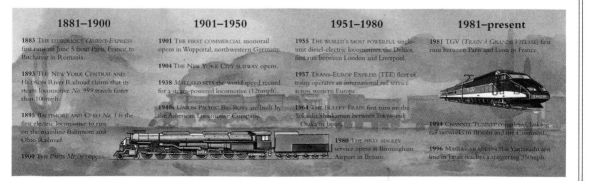

1881–1900	1901–1950	1951–1980	1981–present
1883 The luxurious *Orient-Express* first runs on June 5 from Paris, France, to Bucharest in Romania.	**1901** The first commercial monorail opens in Wuppertal, northwestern Germany.	**1955** The world's most powerful single-unit diesel-electric locomotives, the Deltics, first run between London and Liverpool.	**1981** TGV (*Train à Grande Vitesse*) first runs between Paris and Lyon in France.
1893 The New York Central and Hudson River Railroad claims that its steam locomotive No. 999 travels faster than 100mph.	**1904** The New York City subway opens.	**1957** Trans-Europ Express (TEE) fleet of trains operates an international rail service across western Europe.	
	1938 *Mallard* sets the world speed record for a steam-powered locomotive (126mph).		**1994** Channel Tunnel completed, linking rail networks in Britain and the Continent.
1895 Baltimore and Ohio No. 1 is the first electric locomotive to run on the mainline Baltimore and Ohio Railroad.	**1940s** Union Pacific Big Boys are built by the American Locomotive Company.	**1964** The Bullet Train first runs on the Tokaido Shinkansen between Tokyo and Osaka in Japan.	
1900 The Paris Metro opens.		**1980** The first Maglev service opens at Birmingham Airport in Britain.	**1996** Maglev train on the Yamanashi test line in Japan reaches a staggering 350mph.

RAILROAD TRACK

A FULLY LADEN freight or passenger train is heavy, so the track it runs on has to be tough. Today, rails are made from steel, which is a much stronger material than the cast iron used for the first railroads. The shape of the rail also helps to make it tough. If you sliced through a rail from top to bottom you would see it has an "I"-shaped cross section. The broad, flat bottom narrows into the "waist" of the I and widens again into a curved head. Most countries use a rail shaped like this.

Tracks are made up of lengths of rail, which are laid on wooden or concrete crossbeams called ties. Train wheels are a set distance apart, so rails must be a set distance apart, too. The distance between rails is called the gauge. In Britain, the gauge was fixed at 4ft 8½in in the mid-1800s. Before then, the width of trains and gauges varied from one rail network to the next. So a train from one rail network could not run over the lines of another rail network.

Hard labor
Laying rail track is backbreaking work. Up until the mid-1900s, it was always done by hand. The ground is leveled first. Then crushed rock is laid to form a solid base before the ties are put into position. The rails rest on metal baseplates to hold them firm. The baseplates are secured to the ties either by spikes (big nails), track bolts or large metal spring-clips. Today, machines are used to lay track in most countries, although some countries still use manual labor.

MAKING TRACKS

You will need: two sheets of stiff card measuring 10¼ x 4⅛in, pencil, ruler, scissors, glue and glue brush, silver and brown paint, paintbrush, water pot, one sheet of foam board measuring 8 x 5in, one sheet of paper (11 x 8½in), masking tape, one sheet of thin card measuring 4 x 2in.

1 Place one 10¼ x 4⅛in piece of card lengthwise. Draw a line ⅛in in from each of the outside edges. Draw two more lines, each 1⅜ in from the outside edges. This is side A.

2 Turn the card over (side B) and place it lengthwise. Measure and draw lines 1⅛in and 1⅜in in from each edge. Repeat steps 1 and 2 with the second piece of 10½ x 4¼cm card.

3 Hold the ruler firmly against one of the lines you have drawn. Use the tip of a pair of scissors to score along the line. Repeat for all lines on both sides of both pieces of card.

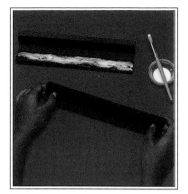

4 Place the cards A side up. For each one in turn, fold firmly along the two pairs of outer lines. Fold up from the scored side. Turn the card over. Repeat for inner lines.

5 With the A side up, press the folds into the I-shape of the rail. Open out again. Glue the B side of the ⅜in-wide middle section as shown. Repeat for the second rail.

6 Give your two rails a metallic look by painting the upper (A) sides silver. Leave the paint to dry, then apply a second coat. Leave the second coat to dry.

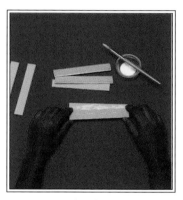

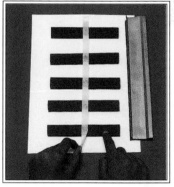

7 Use a pencil and ruler to mark out ten 5 x ⅜in strips on the foam board. Cut them out. Glue two strips together to make five thick railroad ties. Leave them to dry.

8 Paint the ties brown on their tops and sides to make them look like wood. Leave them to dry, then apply a second coat of paint. Leave the second coat to dry, too.

9 Lay the ties on a piece of paper, 1¾₆in apart. Run a strip of masking tape down the middle to hold them in place.

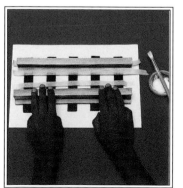

10 Glue the base of one rail and press it into place along the line of ties. The outside edge of the rail should be ⅜in in from the edge of the tie. Glue the other track into position in the same way. Secure the rails in place with masking tape until the glue is dry. Then gently remove all the masking tape.

11 Make at least two sets of rails. These will be able to carry the *Toy Train* and *Brake Van* described in later projects. To join the rails together, roll up the 4 x 2in length of thin card. Insert one end into the top of the I-shape in one rail. Gently push the second rail on to the other end.

STEAMING AHEAD

Horses, oxen or people provided the pulling power for cars on rails and roads for thousands of years. In the 1800s, inventors came up with an alternative. They worked out how to use steam power for pulling wheeled vehicles. In 1825, the world's first public steam railway, the 25-mile-long Stockton and Darlington line, opened in England. On its opening day, the train hauled both freight and passenger cars. Later, it was used mainly for carrying coal. Five years later, the Liverpool and Manchester line opened with its new, steam-driven passenger trains. The company had run a competition called the Rainhill Trials to find the best locomotive for its railway. Both horse-drawn and steam locomotives took part. The steam-driven *Rocket* won.

The success of the *Rocket* convinced investors to back the development of steam-powered locomotives. The brains behind the *Rocket* and the Stockton and Darlington and Liverpool and Manchester railways were George Stephenson and his son Robert. In 1823, they set up the world's first locomotive factory. Other British engineers began to experiment with steam power, and locomotives were made for use in Britain and around the world.

Race to success
The *Rocket,* designed and built by George and Robert Stephenson, convinced people that steam power was better than horse power. At the Rainhill Trials in 1829, the *Rocket* traveled 70 miles at an average speed of 15mph.

Slow train to China
This Chinese locomotive is a KD class, which followed an American design. The Chinese did not make their own locomotives until they began to set up their own factories in the 1950s. Before then, locomotives had been imported from countries such as the USA, Britain, and Japan. Some Chinese trains are still steam-driven today, although diesel and electric ones are rapidly replacing them.

hot gases pass through to boiler

firebox

cab

regulator valve

boiler tubes surrounded by water

engine

steam passes through pipes into cylinders

smokestack

smokebox

steam valve

piston inside cylinder

driving wheels

coupling rod

connecting rod

leading truck

Steam traction

A steam engine converts the energy released from combustion into kinetic energy or movement. First, fuel (most often coal) is burned in a firebox to produce hot gases. The gases pass through boiler tubes that run the length of the water-filled boiler. The hot, gas-filled tubes heat the surrounding water and turn it into steam. This steam passes into cylinders, each of which contains a close-fitting piston. The steam pushes the piston along. The steam then escapes via a valve (one-way opening), and the piston can move back again. Rods connect the piston to the wheels. As the piston moves back and forth, it moves the rods, which, in turn, make the wheels go around.

FACT BOX

• Steam locomotives need about 26gal of water for every mile they travel. It takes 26–55lb of coal—equivalent to seven or eight times the weight of the water—to turn the water into steam.

The Big Boys

In the 1940s, American engineers were designing huge steam locomotives such as this Union Pacific Challenger. At more than 130ft, the Union Pacific's Big Boys were the world's longest-ever steam locomotives—more than five times the length of the Stephensons' *Rocket*. They could haul long passenger or freight trains speedily across the USA's vast landscape.

Big wheels

The Stirling Single locomotive had only one pair of large driving wheels (third in from the left). The driving wheels are driven directly by the piston and connecting rod from the cylinder. Most steam locomotives had two or more pairs of driving wheels linked by coupling rods. The Single, designed by British engineer Patrick Stirling in the 1870s, reached speeds of 80mph.

BEARING THE LOAD

THE VEHICLE and machinery carried by a modern locomotive's underframe and wheels may weigh up to 110 tons. As bigger and more powerful locomotives were built, more wheels were added to carry the extra weight. Early steam locomotives such as the Stephensons' *Rocket* had only two pairs of wheels. Most steam locomotives had two, three, or four pairs of driving wheels, all of which turn in response to power from the cylinders. The cylinders house the pistons, whose movement pushes the driving wheels around via a connecting rod.

The other wheels are connected to the driving wheel by a coupling rod, so that they turn at the same time. The pair of wheels in front of the driving wheels are called the leading truck. The ones behind are the trailing wheels. Locomotives are defined by the total number of wheels they have. For example, a 4-4-0 type locomotive has four leading, four driving, and no trailing wheels.

Staying power
The coupling rod that connects the driving wheel to the other wheels is the lowest of the three rods in this picture. The connecting rod just above links the driving wheel with the cylinder. To stop train wheels from slipping sideways and falling off the rails, there is a rim called the flange on the inside of each wheel. This is a little different from the wheels you will make in this project, which have two flanges so that they sit snugly on the model rails from the *Making Tracks* project.

MAKE AN UNDERFRAME

You will need: sheet of stiff card (22 x 17in), pencil, ruler, pair of compasses, scissors, glue and glue brush, masking tape, four 4in lengths of ⅜in diameter dowel, four pieces of 2 x 2in thin card, silver and black paint, paintbrush, water pot, four map pins.

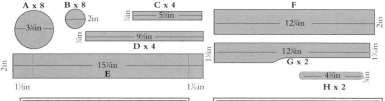

1 Draw and cut out the templates from the stiff card. Use a pair of compasses to draw the wheel templates A and B.

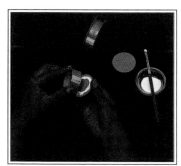

2 Roll the rim templates C and D into rings. Glue and tape to hold. Glue each small wheel circle onto either side of a small ring as shown. Repeat for big wheels. Leave to dry.

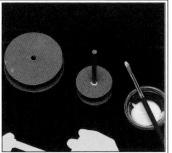

3 Use a pencil to enlarge the compass hole on one side of each wheel. Glue one end of each piece of dowel. Push the dowels into the holes of two big and two small wheels.

4 Roll the 2 x 2in card into sleeves to fit loosely over each piece of dowel. Tape to hold. Make wheel pairs by fixing the remaining wheels on to the dowel as described in step 3.

5 When the glue is dry, paint all four pairs of wheels silver. You do not need to paint the dowel axles. Paint two coats, letting the first dry before you apply the second.

6 Use a ruler and pencil to mark eight equal segments on the outside of each wheel. Paint a small circle over the compass hole, and the center of each segment black.

7 Fold along the dotted lines on E. Glue all three straight edges of template G and stick to template E. Repeat this for the other side. Secure all joins with masking tape.

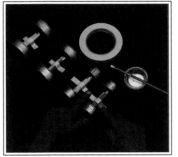

8 Glue the open edges of the underframe. Fit template F on top and hold until firm. Tape over the joins. Give the underframe two coats of black paint. Leave to dry.

9 Glue the card sleeves on to the base of the underframe. Small wheel axles go 1⁷⁄₁₆ and 2¾in from the front, big wheels 1⅜in and 5in from the back. Tape to secure.

10 Give the coupling rods (H) two coats of silver paint. Let the paint dry between coats.

11 Press a map pin through each end of the coupling rods, about ⅜in from edge. Carefully press the pin into each big wheel about ⅜in beneath the center.

12 The wheels on this underframe are arranged for a 4-4-0 type locomotive. You will be able to run the underframe along the model tracks you made in the *Making Tracks* project. The wheels will fit on the rails just like those of a real train. In real locomotives, however, the wheels are mounted on swiveling units called trucks. When the train comes to a curve in the track, the trucks move to allow the train to follow the curve. Each truck has four to six wheels.

DIESEL AND ELECTRIC POWER

TODAY, MOST high-speed trains are either diesel, electric, or a combination of the two. Diesel and electric trains are far more fuel-efficient, cost less to run, and can stop or speed up more quickly than steam trains. Electric trains are also better for the environment, because they do not give off polluting exhaust fumes.

The first electric locomotive ran in 1879 at an exhibition in Berlin in Germany. However, it was another 20 or so years before railroad companies began to introduce electric trains into regular service. Similarly, the first reliable diesel engine was demonstrated in 1889 by its inventor, the French-born German Rudolf Diesel. It took a further 25 years for railroad engineers to design the first practical diesel locomotives. Diesel trains entered regular service during the 1920s in the USA, and during the 1930s in Britain. Steam locomotives were last used regularly in the USA in 1960, in 1968 in Britain, and in 1977 in West Germany.

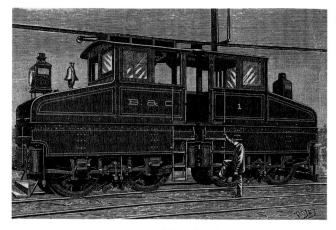

Electric pioneer
In 1895, the B&O *No. 1* became the world's first electric locomotive to run on a mainline track. It entered service in Baltimore in the USA (B&O is short for Baltimore and Ohio Railroad). The route of the B&O *No. 1* took it through many tunnels. One of the advantages of electric locomotives is that, unlike steam trains, they do not fill tunnels and cars with steam and smoke.

Beautiful Bugattis
Racing-car designer Ettore Bugatti designed this diesel train for the French *État* and Paris Lyons *Méditerranée* railroads. In the early 1930s, Bugatti's first trains were diesel or gas single railcars (self-propelled passenger cars). Instead of being hauled by a locomotive, the railcar had its own engine. The railcar-and-car combination shown left was a later introduction. Bugatti came up with the train's streamlined shape by testing his designs in wind tunnels. In 1935, one of Bugatti's trains reached 122mph, setting a world diesel train speed record.

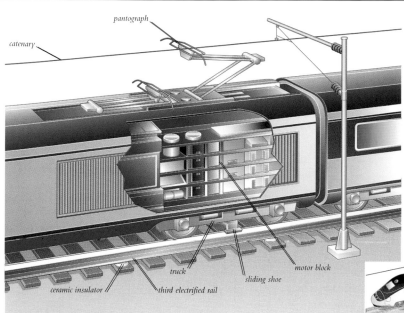

pantograph

catenary

truck

ceramic insulator

third electrified rail

sliding shoe

motor block

Picking up power

Electric locomotives are powered in one of two ways. Some draw electricity from a catenary (overhead cable). This is connected to the locomotive by an "arm" called a pantograph on the roof. Others draw power from a third rail. The locomotive connects to the rail by a device called a shoe. The Eurostar trains that operate in Europe can use either power source depending on what country they are traveling through.

Long-distance runner

Australian National Railways' diesel-electric engines work the long Indian Pacific route. This transcontinental railroad runs between Perth, on the Indian Ocean, and Sydney, on the Pacific Ocean. These locomotives belong to the CL class that was introduced in 1970. This class was based on one that originated in the USA but was built in Sydney, Australia.

Dutch double decker

Dutch Railways' IRM (*InterRegio Materiel*) electric trains are double-decked to cater for high levels of traffic in the densely populated Netherlands. Passenger traffic is expected to rise rapidly, and so the Netherlands is investing heavily in its railroads. Speeds on existing lines are limited to 87mph, but new lines are being built for speeds of up to 137mph.

Cisalpino Pendolino

Italy has developed a tilting train, or pendolino, called the ETR (*Elletro Treni Rapidi*) 470 Cisalpino. These dual-voltage trains are operated by an Italian-Swiss consortium (group of companies). Services began in September 1996 between Italy and Switzerland. The ETR 470 Cisalpino has been developed to be able to use existing rail networks at higher speeds by tilting into the curves as it travels. As a result, the top service speed of these trains is 155mph.

MAPPING THE RAILROADS

Trains cannot easily climb mountains or cope with sharp corners. Planning and mapping the route of a railroad is not simply a matter of drawing a straight line between two destinations. New routes have to be worked out carefully, so that difficult terrain is avoided and time and money will not be wasted on tunnel- or bridge-building. Geographically accurate maps are made before work starts to show every bend of the planned track and the height of the land it will run through. Once construction starts, separate teams of workers may be building sections of track in different parts of the country. The maps are essential to make sure they are all following the same route and will join up when the separate parts meet.

Passengers do not need such detailed maps. They just need to find out which train to catch to get to the place they want to go. They do not need to know each curve or bridge along the way, just the names of the stations. Passenger maps provide a simplified version of the railroad routes, or sometimes a diagram.

Early American railroad
A train runs along the Mohawk and Hudson Railroad, New York State, in the USA. This railroad line opened in 1831 and was built to replace part of the 40-mile route of the Erie Canal. This section of the canal had several locks, which caused delays to the barges. The journey took half the time it had taken by canal.

Railroads in the Wild West
You can see how the railroads often followed a similar route to the wagon trails, passing through mountain passes or river valleys. After the first east-to-west-coast railroad was completed (the Central Pacific Railroad joined the Union Pacific Railroad in 1869), people could cross the continent in just ten days.

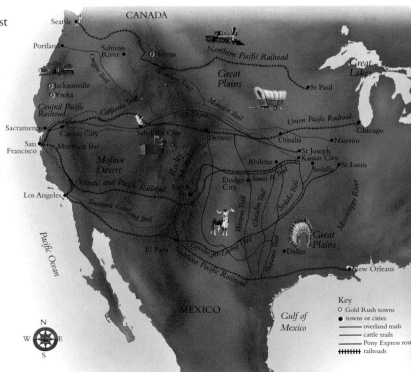

Neat networking

India's massive railroad network was one of the best planned in Asia thanks in large part to the British influence in the region. The Great Indian Peninsular Railway (GIPR) company was the first to open a line, a 25-mile stretch between Bombay and Thana in April 1853. India is a vast country, and railroad engineers had to plan routes for thousands of miles of track. They also had to find ways of taking railroads across every kind of difficult terrain, from boggy marshes to arid deserts, high mountains and deep ravines.

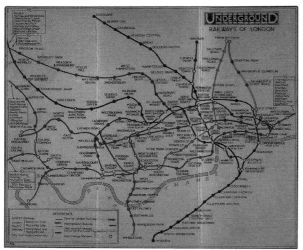

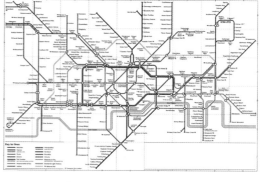

Designing ideas

Apart from the color-coded routes, the 1927 map of the London Underground (at left) looks very different from the one of today (shown above). Early route maps were hard to follow because they tried to show the real geographical route of lines. More abstract, diagrammatical maps were the brainwave of British engineering draughtsman Henry C. Beck. His 1933 redesign of the London Underground map was inspired by electrical circuit diagrams. It makes no attempt to show the real geographical route and is not drawn to scale.

Surveying railroad lines

Today, computer programs are used to plan and design new railroad routes. Data collected from on-the-ground surveying equipment (shown here), or the latest high-tech global positioning systems, is fed into a computer. The information is analyzed to insure that the new rail route is feasible. The most direct route is not always the cheapest. Surveyors must consider factors such as difficult terrain, environmental benefits, and existing rail networks when planning new routes.

BUILDING RAILROADS

THERE WERE no automatic tools or building machines in the 1800s when the first railroads were built. Everything was done by hand. Gangs of laborers moved mountains of earth using nothing but picks, shovels, and barrows. Horses pulled the heaviest loads. Never before had so much earth been shifted, or so many bridges or tunnels built.

The challenge for the engineers who planned the railroads was to construct tracks that were as level as possible. In the early days, locomotives had difficulty climbing even the slightest slope.

Channels were dug or blasted through low hills, while mounds of earth and rock were piled into embankments to carry tracks over boggy or low ground. The railroad routes had to avoid crossing high mountains and deep valleys. Sometimes, though, there was no getting around these obstacles. In the late 1800s, engineers such as Isambard Kingdom Brunel in Britain and Gustave Eiffel in France, began to design tunnels and bridges that were longer and stronger than the world had ever known.

Army on the march
Railroads were carved out of the landscape during the 1800s by gangs of strong laborers. Originally, these workmen built navigations, or channels, equipped with little more than picks and shovels. Gangs often moved from place to place, as one track, tunnel or bridge was completed and work on a new one started up. Some of the workers lived in temporary camps, while others rented rooms in nearby towns. The laborers had strong muscles, but many were also skilled carpenters, miners, stonemasons, or blacksmiths.

The best route
Millions of tons of earth and rock were blasted away for channels and to make railroad routes as level and as straight as possible. Even modern trains slow down on hills. Early steam locomotives just ground to a halt. Sharp curves would cause trains to derail. Alfred Nobel's development of dynamite in 1866 made blasting safer. It was more stable than earlier explosives.

FACT BOX
• At nearly 34 miles long, the Seikan Tunnel in Japan is presently the world's longest railroad tunnel. The Alp Transit Link between Switzerland and Italy will beat this record by 2 miles. This tunnel is due to be completed in 2012.

• The world's longest double-decker road and railroad suspension bridge is also in Japan. Called the Minami Bisan-seto Bridge, its main span is just over 1,200 yards long.

Bridging the valleys

There is not one perfect design for any bridge. In each case, an engineer has to take many factors into consideration before making the decision. These include the weight and frequency of traffic over the bridge, whether the underlying rock is hard or soft, the bridge's appearance in the landscape, and the overall cost of the project.

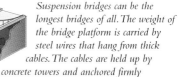

Suspension bridges can be the longest bridges of all. The weight of the bridge platform is carried by steel wires that hang from thick cables. The cables are held up by concrete towers and anchored firmly at the valley sides.

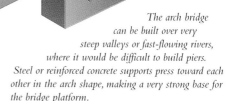

The beam bridge is made up of a horizontal platform supported on two or more piers (pillars). Sometimes a framework of steel girders is added. The girders act as a brace to strengthen and support the beam bridge between its piers.

The arch bridge can be built over very steep valleys or fast-flowing rivers, where it would be difficult to build piers. Steel or reinforced concrete supports press toward each other in the arch shape, making a very strong base for the bridge platform.

Building workers

Thousands of skilled workers are involved in the manufacture of locomotives and rolling stock (passenger cars and freight cars). There are whole factories that specialize in making particular parts of the engine or carriage, such as buffers or electric motors. At this factory, wheels and axles are being put together to be fitted to the truck. Today, much of the work is carried out by machines, but some tasks, such as precision welding (joining of metal parts), still have to be done by hand.

Machines lighten the load

A Paved Concrete Track (PACT for short) machine is one way of taking the sweat out of laying railroad track. It lays a trackbed of continuous concrete. Then, when the concrete is dry, other machines lift and clip the metal rails on top. In another automated method of track-laying, complete sections of track are made in factories with the rails already fixed to concrete ties. They are then transported to the site and lifted into position by cranes. Machines that could do such jobs automatically were introduced in the mid-1900s. They allowed the work to be done much more quickly, involving fewer people and a lot less effort.

LOAD–BEARING TUNNEL

TUNNELS OFTEN have to bear the weight of millions of tons of rocks and earth—or even water—above them. One way of preventing the tunnel collapsing is to make a continuous brick arch run along the length of the tunnel. Wedge-shaped keystones at the peak of the arch lock the whole structure together and support the arch and everything else above it. An arched roof is much stronger than a flat roof, because any weight above the tunnel is passed down through the sides of the arch and out toward the ground.

Between 1872 and 1882, a 9⅓-mile-long railway tunnel was driven through Europe's highest mountains, the Alps, to link Switzerland to northern Italy. The St. Gotthard tunnel was the greatest achievement in tunnel engineering of the time. Today, a long, train-like machine is used to build tunnels such as the Channel Tunnel. A big drill carves out the hole, sending the spoil backward on a conveyor belt. Behind it, robotic cranes lift precast concrete sections of the tunnel into place.

Keystone is key
Before a tunnel is built, engineers have to make sure the rock and soil are easy to cut through but firm enough not to collapse. A framework is used to build brick arches. The bricks are laid around both sides of the framework up toward the center. When the central keystone is in place, the arch will support itself and the framework can be removed.

SUPPORTING ARCH

You will need: *two wooden building blocks or house bricks, two pieces of thick card (width roughly the same as the length of the blocks or bricks), a few heavy pebbles.*

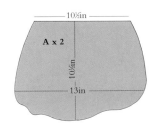

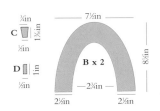

1 Place one of the pieces of card on top of the building blocks. Place pebbles on top as shown above. You will see that the tunnel roof sags under the weight.

2 Curve a second piece of card under the flat roof as shown. The roof supports the weight of the pebbles because the arch supports the flat section, making it stronger.

KEYSTONE

You will need: *masking tape, piece of thick card measuring 18 x 10½in, two sheets of thick card measuring 14¼ x 12in, ruler, pencil, scissors, piece of thin card measuring 17¼ x 16in, newspaper, cup of flour, ½ cup of water, acrylic paints, paintbrush, water pot, piece of thin card (11 x 8½in), glue and glue brush.*

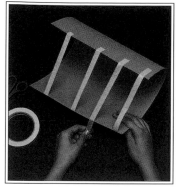

1 Tear off about four long strips of masking tape. Curve the 18 x 10½in rectangle of card lengthwise. Use the tape to hold the curve in place as shown above.

2 Copy the two templates A on to two 14½ x 12in pieces of thick card. Cut out the shapes. Attach each one to the sides of the tunnel and secure with tape as shown above.

3 Fold the 17¼ x 16in thin card in half. Copy the arch template B on to the card. Cut out to make two tunnel entrances. Stick these to the tunnel with masking tape as shown.

4 Scrunch newspaper into balls and tape to the tunnel and landscape. Mix the flour and water to make a thick paste. Dip newspaper strips in the paste. Layer them over the tunnel.

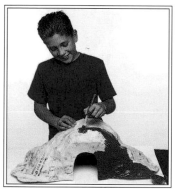

5 Leave to dry. When completely dry and hard, remove the tape and paint the tunnel and landscape green. Apply three coats, letting each one dry before you apply the next.

6 Paint the 11 x 8½in thin card to look like bricks. Draw and cut out templates C and D. Draw around C to make two keystones and D to make lots of bricks. Carefully cut the shapes out.

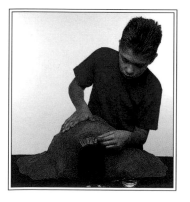

7 When the paint is dry, glue the keystones at the very top of each tunnel entrance. Then glue bricks around the arch either side of the keystone as shown. In a real tunnel, there would have been lots of central keystones running along the length of the tunnel.

8 Add finishing touches to your model using brown and green paints. Scrunch up newspaper into balls and dip them in the paste to make fake bushes. Leave them to dry and then paint them with brown and green paints. Do at least two or three coats. Leave them to dry between coats.

STATION STOP

ONCE PASSENGER trains began running in the 1830s, people needed special buildings where they could buy tickets and shelter from the weather while they waited to board. No one had ever designed or built train stations before. The owners of the new railroad companies wanted to make as much money as possible, so they had big, impressive mainline stations built to attract customers. Long platforms were essential for trains with many cars, so that passengers could get on and off trains safely. There also had to be waiting rooms and restaurants, as well as offices where station staff worked.

London's Euston Station was the first to have separate platforms for arrivals and departures. This train station was also among the earliest to have a metal and glass roof over the platforms. Euston was opened in 1838. From then on, most big train stations had glass and metal roofs. They were relatively cheap and easy to build, and they also let in a lot of daylight, which helped to save money on artificial lighting. In those days, lighting was provided by expensive gas lamps.

Housed in style
An early steam train puffs out of the first circular roundhouses, built in 1847 in London. Even the roundhouses where steam locomotives were housed for maintenance or repair were well designed. In the middle of these circular sheds was a turntable with short sections of track arranged around it, rather like the spokes of a wheel. Locomotives were parked on each section of track and released when they were needed for a journey.

Decorative ironwork
The iron pillars of stations in the 1900s were cast into a fantastic variety of shapes and then beautifully painted. At this time, cast iron was one of the latest building materials. Cast-iron pillars and arches were fairly cheap and quick to erect, as well as being a strong framework for station walls and roofs.

Temples of fashion
Bristol Temple Meads Station, Britain, looked like this in the 1800s. Engineers and architects tried to make their train stations stylish as well as be functional. During the 1800s, it was fashionable to copy the great building styles of the past. Bristol Temple Meads Station imitated the magnificent Gothic cathedrals and churches of medieval times. Small country stations, on the other hand, often looked like cottages or suburban villas.

Classical train station

The main station building of Washington Union Station in the USA is typical of train stations built in the early 1900s. It has a lofty vaulted ceiling and interiors made of paneled wood. It was opened in 1907 and was built by the Washington Terminal Company, which was specially formed by railroad companies serving the city.

German hub

Busy Cologne *Hauptbahnhof* (main train station) is at the center of Germany's vast rail network in the northwest of the country. The old steel-and-glass train shed was damaged during World War II (1939–45) but was later rebuilt. The front of the station has today been completely rebuilt with a more modern frontage.

Simple fare

Unlike the train stations that serve cities, country train stations are often very basic, such as this one at Pargothan, India. There are no platforms, and passengers climb into the trains from the track.

Single span

Atocha is the terminal of Spain's *Alta Velocita Española* (AVE) high-speed rail link between the capital, Madrid, and Seville in southern Spain. It was built in the early 1890s, and it serves all routes to the south, east and southeast of Madrid. It is Spain's largest train station and is famous for its single-span arched roof.

FACT BOX
• The world's largest train station is Beijing West Railway Station in China. It covers 133 acres and is bigger than the world's smallest country, the Vatican City in Rome, Italy.

• The world's highest train station is at Condor in Bolivia, South America. It is at 15,702ft above sea level, 1,010ft higher than the Matterhorn Mountain in the Alps.

• The world's busiest train station is Clapham Junction in south London, Britain. More than 2,000 trains pass through the station every 24 hours.

SHRINKING WORLD

Ticket to ride
Cheap, speedy trains meant that for the first time ordinary people, rather than the wealthy, could travel for pleasure. Train companies began offering day-excursion trips in the early 1830s. Outings to the seaside were particularly popular.

Ceremonial spike
On May 10, 1869, a golden spike was hammered into the track when the world's first transcontinental railroad was completed, linking the east and west coasts of the USA. The railroad was built by two companies, and the spike marked the meeting place of the two tracks at Promontory Summit in Utah.

BEFORE THE coming of the railroads, the fastest way to travel was on horseback. Even though the swiftest racehorse can gallop at more than 37mph, it cannot keep this speed up for longer than a few minutes. Trains, on the other hand, can travel at high speed for hours on end. They can also transport hundreds of people at a time, or tens of carloads of freight, across vast distances. As more and more railroad lines began snaking across the countryside, life speeded up and the world seemed to grow smaller. People and goods could reach places they had never been to before.

During the 1800s, railroad technology spread from Britain all over the world. Tracks were laid between towns and cities at first. Later, railroads slowly grew to link countries and span continents. The world's first transcontinental railroad was completed in the USA in 1869. The expansion of the railroad system in the USA was rapid. Railroads were built through areas that had not yet been settled and played an important part in opening up many parts of the country.

FACT BOX
• With more than 149,000 miles of rail track, the USA has the world's longest network of railroads—just about enough to wrap around the Equator six times.

• It takes just over eight days to ride the entire length of the world's longest railroad, the Trans-Siberian line in Asia. This railroad, which opened in 1903, runs for 5,972 miles from Moscow to Vladivostok.

Desert runner
When surveyors planned the western section of Australia's transcontinental railroad, they plotted what is still the world's longest stretch of straight track. This 297-mile section lies within a vast, treeless desert called the Nullarbor Plain between Port Augusta and Kalgoorlie in southwestern Australia. The western section of this transcontinental railroad opened in 1917. The luxury Indian Pacific service was launched in 1969. Today, the 2,461-mile journey from Sydney to Perth takes just under three days.

Ruling by rail

A steam train passes over a bridge in India. During the 1800s, the British gradually introduced railroad networks to India and other countries in the British Empire. By speeding up the movement of government officials and the military, trains helped Britain keep control of its empire. Trade goods could be moved more quickly, too, which benefited British-owned companies. By 1939, India had more than 31,000 miles of track.

Keeping up with the times

The time in any place in the world is calculated from Greenwich Mean Time, which is the local time at 0 degrees longitude at Greenwich in London, England. Local time in other countries is calculated as either behind or in front of Greenwich Mean Time. Before the railroads, even cities within the same country kept their own local time, and accurate timetables were impossible. Timekeeping had to be standardized if people were to know when to catch their trains. British railroad companies standardized timekeeping using Greenwich Mean Time in 1847.

Coast-to-coast challenge

Pulled by diesel locomotives, passenger trains can today make the spectacular 2,890-mile journey across Canada in three days. When the Canadian Pacific transcontinental railroad was completed in 1887, the trip took steam trains about a week. The biggest challenge for the army of workers who built the railroad was taking the track through the Rocky Mountains—at Kicking Horse Pass, it climbs to 5,328ft.

A PASSION FOR TRAINS

I N 1830, a young British actress called Fanny Kemble wrote to a friend about her railroad journey pulled by a "brave little she-dragon … the magical machine with its wonderful flying white breath and rhythmical unvarying pace."

Over the years, all sorts of people—young and old, male and female, rich and poor—have caught Fanny's enthusiasm for trains. Some people love traveling on them, enjoying the scenery flickering past the windows and chatting to the strangers they meet on the journey. Others are happiest when they are standing at the end of a platform, spotting trains and noting down locomotive numbers. Other train buffs spend their spare time building their own private museum of railroad history. They collect anything from old tickets, timetables, and luggage labels, to early signaling equipment, station clocks, and locomotive numberplates. Some people "collect" journeys and take pride in traveling on some of the world's most famous railroads.

Museum piece
You can still ride a real steam train today, although in most countries only where short stretches of line have been preserved. Many classic locomotives of the past are on display in railroad museums. Visitors can usually get close enough to touch, and sometimes they are allowed to climb up inside the engineer's cab. You should never get this close when spotting working trains, however. Always stand well back on the platform, and never climb down onto the track.

Railroad mania
The walls of this train buff's room are decorated with prizes collected during years of hunting through junk shops and rummage sales, and attending specialist auctions. Lamps and many other pieces of railroad and station equipment came onto the market in Britain during the 1960s, when the government closed down hundreds of country railroad stations and branch lines.

Collecting signals

During the late 1900s, many old semaphore signals such as the ones in this picture were made redundant. They were replaced with color-light signals controlled from towers. Much of the old signaling was purchased by Britain's heritage railroads, but a few train buffs bought signals for their gardens. The ones in this picture are Great Western Railroad design signals, dating from the 1940s.

Museum pieces

The Baltimore and Ohio Museum was set up in the city of Baltimore, Maryland, by the Baltimore and Ohio Railroad in 1953. The main exhibits are displayed in a full-circle roundhouse in what used to be the railroad's shops. The exhibits feature a full range of locomotives from the last 180 years. They include a replica of the first American steam locomotive and a recently retired diesel passenger locomotive.

Tickets, please

Railroad tickets and timetables are all collectable items for those who are interested in trains and train journeys. A trainspotter's handbook and a set of railroad timetables are essential equipment for the serious train buff. In many countries, specialist bookshops sell handbooks that list all the working locomotives of the day.

WARNING BOX
• At stations, always stand well back from the platform edge.
• On bridges, never climb up walls or fences to get a better view—move somewhere else.
• Railroad lines sometimes have fences on either side of the track to keep people a safe distance from passing trains. Stand behind the fence—never climb over it.
• Modern trains are fast and make very little noise. If you disregard these simple rules, you will be risking your life.

Number crunching

Locomotives have number plates in much the same way that cars have license plates. The number plate is usually on the front of the engine, as can be seen on the front of this locomotive from the Czech Republic. In many countries, train buffs aim to collect the number of every working locomotive, but with so many locomotives in operation, it is a very time-consuming hobby.

TRAINS IN MINIATURE

MODEL TRAINS are just about as old as steam locomotives. The first ones were not for children, though. They were made for the locomotive manufacturers of the early 1800s to show how the newly invented, full-sized machines worked.

Although most toy trains are miniature versions of the real thing, they come in different scales or sizes. Most are built in O scale, which is $\frac{1}{48}$th the size of the real train. The smallest are Z scale, which is $\frac{1}{220}$th the size of a real train. Z-scale locomotives are small enough to fit inside a matchbox! It is extremely difficult to make accurate models to this small a scale, so Z-scale train sets are usually the hardest to find in stores and the most expensive to buy.

All the exterior working parts of the original are shown on the best model locomotives, from the smokestack on top of the engine to the coupling and connecting rods.

Smile, please
In the early 1900s, a few lucky children owned their own toy train. Some early toy trains had clockwork motors or tiny steam engines. Others were "carpet-runners." These were simply pushed or pulled along the floor.

Top-class toys
One British manufacturer of model trains was Bassett-Lowke, the maker of this fine model of *Princess Elizabeth*. Another manufacturer was Hornby, whose trains first went on sale in the 1920s. Hornby quickly grew into Britain's most popular model. Lionel is probably the leading manufacturer of miniature trains in the USA. All these companies produce many different models of real-life trains.

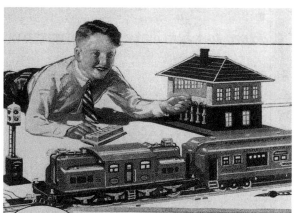

A model world
In the 1920s, toymakers began producing small-scale tabletop model railroads. Train stations and track took up less space than older, larger-scale models had needed. Many of these models were electric-powered and made from cast metal and tin plate by the German firm Bing. Today, these models are very valuable.

The German connection

Model trains are being made at the Fleischmann Train Factory, Nuremberg, Germany. Fleischmann produces highly detailed models of the full range of modern European trains. Like earlier model-railroad manufacturers, Fleischmann does not only make the trains. Collectors and model-railroad buffs can also buy everything that goes to make up a railroad, including signals and towers, lights and level crossings, roundhouses, bridges, and tunnels. There are even train stations and platforms with miniature newspaper stands, station staff, and passengers.

Model behavior

In the earliest train sets, miniature locomotives hauled cars on a never-ending journey around a circular track. Gradually, toymakers began selling more complex layouts, with several sets of track linked by points. Trains could switch from one track to another, just as in real railroads.

Ticket to ride

Model trains come in all sizes, including those that are large enough for children and adults to ride on. These miniature trains have all the working parts and features of their full-sized parents, including a tiny firebox which the engineer stokes with coal to keep the train chuffing along. In the USA in the late 1890s, small-gauge lines were appearing at showgrounds and in amusement parks. By the 1920s, longer miniature railroads were being built in Britain and Germany. Today, many theme parks feature a miniature railroad.

MODEL LOCOMOTIVES

A precision toy

As manufacturing techniques improved, so toy trains became increasingly sophisticated. Today, accurate, working, scale models have all the features of full-size working trains.

TOY TRAINS started to go on sale during the mid-1800s. Early toy trains were made of brightly painted wood, and often had a wooden track to run along. Soon, metal trains went on sale, many of them made from tin plate (thin sheets of iron or steel coated with tin). Some of these metal toy trains had windup clockwork motors. Clockwork toy trains were first sold in the USA during the 1880s. The most sophisticated model trains were steam-powered, with tiny engines fired by methylated-spirit burners. Later model trains were powered by electric motors.

Railroad companies often devised special color schemes, called liveries, for their locomotives and cars. Steam locomotives had brass and copper decoration, and some also carried the company's special logo or badge. Many toy trains are also painted in the livery of a real railroad company. The shape of the locomotive you can make in this project has a cab typical of the real locomotives made in the 1910s.

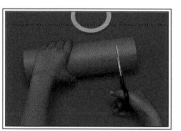

1 Roll the 10¼ x 10¼in card into an 3⅛in diameter tube. Secure it with masking tape. Cut a 2⅛in slit, 2in from one end of the tube.

TOY TRAIN

You will need: *10¼ x 10¼in card, masking tape, scissors, ruler, pencil, 4 x 4in card, glue and glue brush, card for templates, paints, paintbrush, water pot, underframe from earlier project, two thumbtacks, 4½ x ½in red card, split pin.*

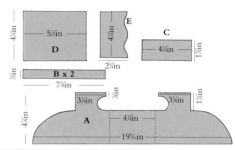

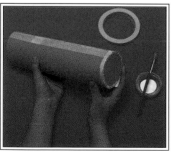

2 Hold the tube upright on the 4 x 4in piece of card. Draw around it. Cut this circle out. Glue the circle to the tube end farthest away from the slit. Tape to secure.

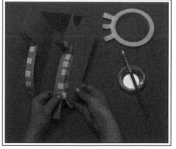

3 Copy and cut out templates. Fold template A along the dotted lines. Fold templates B across, 1⅛in from one end. Glue both strips to the cab as shown and secure with tape.

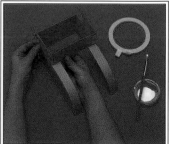

4 When the glue is dry, gently peel off the masking tape. Now glue on template C as shown above. Hold it in place with masking tape until the glue dries.

5 Apply two coats of green paint to the outside of the locomotive. Let the first coat dry before applying the second. Then paint the black parts. Add the red and gold last.

6 Glue around the bottom edge of the cab front C. Put a little glue over the slit in the tube. Fit the front of the cab into the slit. Leave the locomotive to one side to dry.

7 Give roof template D two coats of black paint. Let the paint dry between coats. Glue the top edges of the cab, and place the black roof on top. Leave until dry and firm.

8 Glue the bottom of the cylindrical part of the train to the underframe you made in the *Underframe* project. Press thumbtacks into back of cab and underframe.

9 Glue both sides of one end of the red strip. Slot this between the underframe and the cab, between the thumbtacks. When firm, fold the strip and insert the split pin.

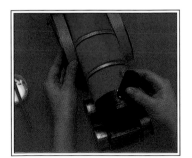

10 Paint one side of template E black. When dry, roll into a tube, and secure with masking tape. Glue wavy edge and secure to front of locomotive as shown above.

Just like a real locomotive, the basic color of your model train has been enhanced with red, black, and gold decoration. The locomotive is now ready to run on the railroad line you made in the Making Tracks project. The engineer and fireman would have shared the cab of the locomotive. The engineer controlled the speed of the train, following the signals and track speed restrictions. The fireman insured a good supply of steam by stoking the fire and filling the boiler with water.

SIGNALS AND SIGNALING

THE EARLIEST railroads were single tracks that ran directly between one place and another. Later, more tracks were laid and branched off these main lines. Trains were able to cross from one line to another on movable sections of track called switches.

To avoid crashes, a system of signals was needed to show engineers if the track ahead was clear. The first signalers stood beside the track and waved flags during daylight or lamps at night. From 1841, human signalers were replaced by signals called semaphores on posts with wooden arms.

By 1889, three basics of rail safety were established by law in Britain – block, brake, and lock. Block involved stopping one train until the one in front had passed by. Brakes are an obvious safety feature on passenger trains. Lock meant that switches and signals had to be interlocked, so that a lever in the tower could not be pulled without changing both the switch and the signal.

Hand signals
The first people to be responsible for train safety in Britain were the railway police. The policemen used flags and lamps to direct the movements of trains. In the absence of flags, signals were given by hand. One arm outstretched horizontally meant "line clear," one arm raised meant "caution" and both arms raised meant "danger, stop."

Mechanical signals
A policeman operates a Great Western Railway disk and crossbar signal. The disk and crossbar were at right angles and rotated so the engineer could either see the full face of the disk, meaning "go," or the crossbar, meaning "stop."

Lighting up the night
Electric signals were not used until the 1920s, when color-light signals were introduced. Color-light signals look like road traffic lights. A green light means the track is clear, red shows danger, and yellow means caution. Color-light signals, such as these in France, are accompanied by displays showing the number of the signal, speed restrictions, and other information for engineers.

Signal improvements

This hand-operated signal frame features details dating from the 1850s, when a signaling system called interlocking was introduced. Signals and switches were interlocked (linked) so that a single lever moved a signal and the set of switches it protected at the same time. Tower levers were moved by hand to set signals and switches in those days. In many countries today, signals are set automatically by computers that are housed in a central signaling control room.

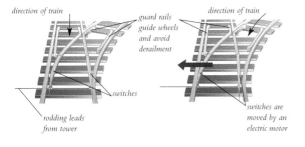

direction of train

guard rails guide wheels and avoid derailment

direction of train

switches

rodding leads from tower

switches are moved by an electric motor

Safety first

Semaphore signals such as these made a major difference to railroad safety when they were introduced during the 1840s. At first, railroad companies throughout the world used semaphore signals with oil lamps behind colored glass to show if the track was clear at night (green light) or at danger (red light). From the 1920s, many countries upgraded their systems by introducing electric color-light signals.

Switches and humpyard

Trains are "switched" from one track to another using switches. Part of the track, called the blade, moves so that the wheels are guided smoothly from one route onto the other. The blade moves as a result of a signaler pulling a lever in the tower. The blade and lever are connected by a system of metal rods, and the lever cannot be pulled unless the signal is clear. From the late 1800s, railroad companies built humpyards. These made it easier to shunt freight cars together to make a freight train. As the cars went over a hump in the yard, they uncoupled. When they went down the hump, they could be switched into different sidings using a set of switches.

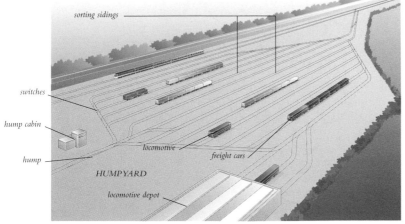

sorting sidings

switches

hump cabin

hump

locomotive

freight cars

HUMPYARD

locomotive depot

SAFETY FIRST

ACCIDENTS ARE a tragic feature of railroad travel today, but trains remain the safest form of land transport in most countries. Modern technology is largely responsible for the improvements in rail safety. In Britain, trains are fitted with an Automatic Warning System (AWS). If the signal indicates that the track ahead is clear, electric magnets between the rails send a message to equipment under the train. This causes a bell to sound in the engineer's cab. If the signal is not clear, the magnet stays "dead," and a horn sounds in the cab. If the engineer does not react, the brakes come on automatically. An improved system, called Train Protection and Warning System (TPWS), uses existing AWS but also provides an automatic stop at a red signal and a speed trap in advance of the signal.

A more advanced system is Automatic Train Protection (ATP). The train picks up electronic messages from the track, and they tell the engineer to slow down or stop. If he or she fails to respond, there is a warning and the brakes come on. ATP also slows or stops the train if it exceeds the speed limit.

On collision course

Head-on crashes were more common in the early days of the railroads, even though there were far fewer trains. On some routes, there was only a single-track line. A train heading toward a station was in danger of meeting another train leaving it. In most countries today, trains are timetabled so that no two are on the same line at the same time. This situation can only arise if a train passes a stop signal at a set of switches.

Japanese crash

A crane lifts a derailed train along the Hanshin Railway near Shinzaike Station. The accident was caused by an earthquake that devastated the city of Kobe on the Japanese island of Honshu in 1995. Several stations and several miles of elevated railroad lines were destroyed on the three main lines that run from Kobe to Osaka.

Control center

From the 1960s, signaling over large areas has been controlled from centralized towers. The towers have a control panel that displays all the routes, signals, and switches that the tower controls. Signalers set up safe routes for trains in the area by operating switches and buttons. Signals work automatically, and the switches change using electronic controls. This insures trains cannot get onto routes where there is an oncoming train. In the most modern signaling centers, the routes appear on computer monitors. The signaler uses a cursor to set up routes instead of using buttons and switches.

train brake controller

brake gauge   *speedometer*   *deadman's button*

In the driving seat

The control desk of a London Underground, or "Tube," train has a number of standard safety features. The train brake controller is a manual control to slow the train. The deadman's button must be pressed down continually by the motorman while the train is moving. If the motorman collapses, the button comes up and the train stops.

Onboard safety

In the event of an emergency, passengers will always find standard safety devices, such as fire extinguishers and first-aid kits, on board a train.

Buffer zone

Buffers stop trains at the end of a line. They are made of metal or wood and metal and are fixed to the track. They are strong enough to absorb much of the energy of a colliding train. Signals control a train's speed so that even if a train collides with the bufferstops, it is usually traveling slowly.

CABOOSE

FEW EARLY steam locomotives had brakes. If the engineer needed to stop quickly, he had to throw the engine into reverse. By the early 1860s, braking systems for steam locomotives had been invented. Some passenger cars also had their own handbrakes that were operated by the conductors. A caboose was added to the back of trains, too, but its brakes were operated by a brakeman riding inside.

The problem was that the engineer had no control over the rest of the train. When he wanted to stop, he had to blow the engine whistle to warn each of the conductors to apply their brakes.

The brakes on a locomotive and its cars or freight cars needed to be linked. This was made possible by the invention of an air-braking system in 1869. When the engineer applies the brakes, compressed air travels along pipes linking all parts of the train and presses brake shoes. Air brakes are now used on nearly all the world's railroads.

Coupling up

A locomotive is joined up to a car by a connection called a coupler. At first, chains or rigid bars were used to join cars. Later, a rigid hook at the end of one vehicle connected to chains on the front of the next. From the late 1800s, couplers made from steel castings and springs were used, but uncoupling was done by hand. Today, passenger trains couple and uncouple automatically.

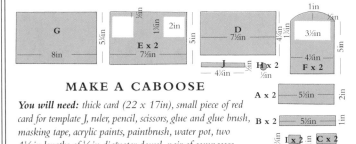

MAKE A CABOOSE

You will need: *thick card (22 x 17in), small piece of red card for template J, ruler, pencil, scissors, glue and glue brush, masking tape, acrylic paints, paintbrush, water pot, two 1¹⁄₁₆in lengths of ³⁄₁₆in diameter dowel, pair of compasses.*

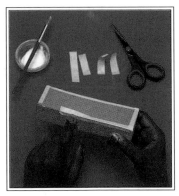

1 Copy the templates on to card and cut them out. Glue templates A, B and C together to make the underframe as shown. Tape over the joins to secure them.

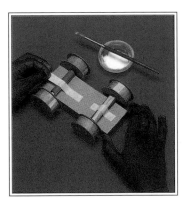

2 Make and paint two pairs of small wheels (diameter 2in) following steps 1 to 5 in the *Underframe* project. Glue and tape the wheel pairs to the underframe.

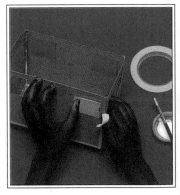

3 Glue the bottom edges of the caboose sides (E) to the caboose base (D). Then glue on the caboose ends (F). Secure the joins with masking tape until the glue is dry.

4 Paint the caboose brown with black details and the wheels and underframe black and silver. Apply two coats of paint, letting each one dry between coats.

5 Paint one side of template G black. Let the paint dry before applying a second coat. Glue the top edges of the caboose. Bend the roof to fit on the top of the caboose.

6 Apply glue to the top surface of the underframe. Stick the caboose centrally on top. Press together until the glue holds firm. Leave to dry completely.

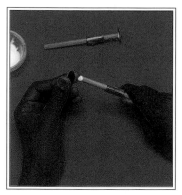

7 Roll up templates I into two ⅜in tubes to fit loosely over the dowel. Tape to hold and paint them silver. Paint the buffer templates H black and stick on each dowel.

8 Use compasses to pierce two holes 1in from each side of the caboose and ⅜in up. Enlarge with a pencil. Glue the end of each dowel buffer. Slot it into the hole. Leave to dry.

9 Cut a slot between the buffers. Fold red card template J in half. Glue each end to form a loop. Push the closed end into the slot. Hold it in place until the glue dries.

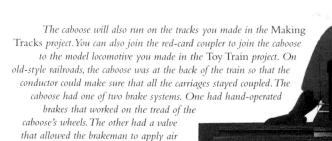

The caboose will also run on the tracks you made in the Making Tracks *project. You can also join the red-card coupler to join the caboose to the model locomotive you made in the* Toy Train *project. On old-style railroads, the caboose was at the back of the train so that the conductor could make sure that all the carriages stayed coupled. The caboose had one of two brake systems. One had hand-operated brakes that worked on the tread of the caboose's wheels. The other had a valve that allowed the brakeman to apply air brakes to all vehicles in the train.*

HAULING FREIGHT

MOST OF the traffic on the world's railroads is made up of freight trains that transport goods such as coal and iron ore from mines and cloth and other manufactured goods from factories. The earliest freight trains were slow because they did not have effective braking systems. Technical developments now mean that freight trains can run much faster than before.

Freight trains made a vast difference to everyday life as the rail networks expanded and brought the country nearer to the city. For the first time, fresh food could be delivered quickly from country farms to city markets. People could also afford to heat their homes. The price of coal for household fires came down because moving coal by train was cheaper and faster than by horse-drawn carts or canal.

In the mid-1900s, motor vehicles and airplanes offered an alternative way of transporting freight. However, concerns about congestion and the environment mean that freight trains continue to be the cheapest, quickest, and most environmentally friendly way of hauling a large volume of freight overland.

Four-legged freight service
The world's first public railroad opened in 1803—for horse-drawn freight cars. The Surrey Iron Railway ran for a little more than 8 miles between Wandsworth and Croydon near London. It went past a number of mills and factories. The factory owners paid a toll to use the railroad and supplied their own horses and cars.

Rolling stock
Freight cars were ramshackle affairs when the first steam trains began running during the 1820s and 1830s. They had metal wheels but, unlike locomotives, they were mainly built from wood. Their design was based on the horse-drawn carts or coal cars they were replacing. Waterproof tarpaulins were tied over goods to protect them from the weather.

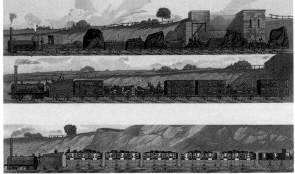

Slow but steady
In the early 1800s, the first steam locomotives hauled coal cars called chaldrons from collieries to ships on nearby rivers. The locomotives were not very powerful. They could pull only a few cars at a time. Going any faster would have been dangerous because neither the locomotives nor the cars had much in the way of brakes!

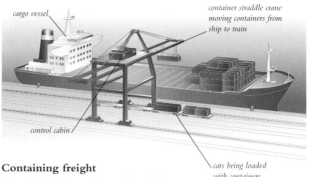

Mail by rail

Railroads first carried mail in the 1830s. A special mail car was introduced in Britain in 1838. Post Office workers on board sorted the mail for delivery while the train was moving. Modern versions of these traveling mail rooms still operate today.

Containing freight

From the 1960s, metal containers like giant boxes have transported goods by sea, rail, and road. They are a way of combining different methods of transporting goods in the most effective way possible. The containers are simply lifted from one vehicle to another using large cranes called straddle cranes. The trains usually have specially designed flatcars onto which the containers are locked into position. The containers remain sealed, apart from when they are inspected by customs officials.

cargo vessel

container straddle crane moving containers from ship to train

control cabin

cars being loaded with containers

FACT BOX

• Today, freight trains haul bulky loads, such as coal, oil, and minerals, in purpose-built cars.

• As many as 10,000 freight trains crisscross the USA every day.

• Some of the world's freight trains have 200 cars and can be up to 2½ miles long.

• Modern diesel and electric freight trains can haul heavy loads at speeds of up to 75 miles.

Bulk transportation

Today, freight trains mainly transport heavy, bulky loads such as coal, iron ore, grain, or building materials. Smaller, lighter goods are usually sent by road or air. Railroad companies pioneered the idea of specially designed vehicles for different types of freight— tankers for liquids such as milk or chemicals, for example, and hoppers that tip sideways for unloading gravel or coal.

Chinese circle

From the mid-1900s, Chinese electric locomotives such as this hauled ore hoppers. The trains carried iron ore to be smelted in blast furnaces on an 50 mile circular line. The locomotives were based on a Swiss design. They had a sloping front so that the driver could see easily from the cab.

GOING UNDERGROUND

Railroad networks made it easier for people to travel from the country to cities and towns to shop or work. During the 1800s, the streets within cities became extremely crowded with people and traffic. One way of coping with the problem of moving around the cities was to tunnel underground.

The world's first passenger subway system opened in 1863. It was the Metropolitan Line between Paddington Station and Farringdon Street in London, Britain. Steam locomotives hauled the passenger cars, and smoke in the tunnels was a big problem. The locomotives were fitted with structures called condensers that were supposed to absorb the smoke, but they did not work properly. Passengers on the trains traveled through a fog-like darkness. Those waiting at the stations choked on the smoke drifting out from the tunnels.

The answer was to use electric trains, and the first underground electric railroad opened in London in 1890. Today, nearly every major city in the world has its own subway system.

Cut-and-cover construction
The first underground passenger railroads were built using a new method called cut-and-cover construction. A large trench—usually 33ft wide by 16ft deep—was cut into the earth along the railroad's proposed route. Then the trench was lined with brickwork and it was roofed over. After that, the streets were re-laid on top of the tunnel.

Tunnel maze
This cross section of the underground system in central London in 1864 shows the proposed route of the new Charing Cross line beneath the existing Metropolitan Line. Deep-level subways were not built until 1890, when developments such as ways of digging deeper tunnels, electric locomotives, better elevators, and escalators became a reality.

Underground shelters
Londoners came up with another use for their city's warren of underground railroad tunnels during World War II (1939–45). They used them as deep shelters from night-time bombing raids. The electric lines were switched off, and people slept wherever they could find enough room to lie down. Canteens were set up on many platforms. More than 130,000 gallons of tea and cocoa were served every night.

Keeping up with the times

The Washington DC Metro in the USA was opened in 1976. It is one of the world's newest and most up-to-date subway systems. The trains have no motormen and the entire network is controlled automatically by a computerized central control system. Passengers traveling in the air-conditioned cars have a smooth, fast ride due to the latest techniques in train and track construction. The airy, 200-yard-long train stations are much more spacious than those built in the early 1900s.

FACT BOX

• The world's busiest subway is in New York City and has 468 train stations. The first section opened in 1904.

• The London Underground is the world's longest subway system. It has nearly 250 miles of track.

• The world's second electric subway system was the 2½-mile-long line in Budapest, Hungary. It opened in 1896.

Overground undergrounds

Work started on the first 6-mile-long section of the Paris *Metro* in 1898 and took over two years to complete. The engineers who designed early underground subways, such as the Paris *Metro,* often found it quicker and easier to take sections above ground, particularly when crossing rivers. The station entrances were designed by French architect Hector Guimard in the then-fashionable Art Nouveau style. They made the Paris *Metro* one of the most distinctive and stylish subway systems in the world.

Mechanical earthworm

The cutting head of a Tunnel-Boring Machine (TBM), which was used to bore the Channel Tunnel between England and France. The 26ft-wide cutting head is covered with diamond-studded teeth. As the TBM rotates, the teeth rip through the earth. The waste material, or spoil, falls onto a conveyor belt and is transported to the surface. The cutting head grips against the sides of the tunnel and inches farther forward under the pressure of huge rams. As the tunnel is cut, cranes line the tunnel with curved concrete segments that arrive on conveyors at the top and bottom of the TBM.

RIDING HIGH

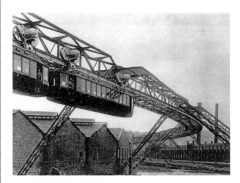

Wonder of Wuppertal
The oldest working monorail in the world is located in Wuppertal, Germany. Almost 20 million passengers have traveled along the 8-mile-long route since it opened in 1901. It is suspended about 33ft above the ground. The wheels run along the top of the rail.

IN SOME of the world's cities, the solution to overcrowded streets was to build railway networks above ground level. The earliest kind of overhead trains ran on a twin-rail track. The track was raised above the ground on arching, viaduct-like supports. These "elevated railways" were built in several American and European cities from the mid-1800s onward.

Today, some overhead trains run along a single rail called a monorail. Some are suspended systems in which the train hangs beneath the rail. Others are straddle systems in which the train sits over the rail.

Twin-rail systems called Light Rapid Transit (LRT) are now more common than monorails. They are described as "light" because they carry fewer people and therefore need lighter-weight vehicles and track than mainline, or "heavy," railways. In many cities, LRT cars are like a cross between a streetcar and a train. They run on rails through town and city streets, as well as through underground tunnels and along elevated tracks.

Flying train
Inventor George Bennie's experimental monorail was one of the strangest ever built. The streamlined machine was named the Railplane. It had airplane propellers front and back to thrust it along. It first "flew" in July 1930, along a 44-yard-long test line over a railroad track near Glasgow in Scotland.

Climb every mountain
The Paris funicular climbs to the city's highest point, the top of Montmartre. Funiculars were invented during the 1800s and are used to move cars up and down hillsides or steep slopes. Usually, there are two parallel tracks. Each one has a passenger-carrying car attached. In the early days, each car carried a large water tank that was filled with water at the top of the slope and emptied at the bottom. The extra weight of the car going down pulled the lighter car up. Later funiculars have winding drums powered by electricity to haul a cable up and down.

Tomorrow's world

During the 1950s, American film producer Walt Disney wanted to have a monorail for his futuristic Tomorrowland attraction when he built his first Disneyland theme park in California. The monorail opened in 1959 and was an immediate success with visitors. Disney was trying to promote monorails as the transportation system of the future, but his railroad had just the opposite effect. For many years, monorails were seen as little more than amusement-park rides.

Not everyone's darling

The monorail system in Sydney, Australia, links the heart of the city to a tourist development in nearby Darling Harbour. It has proved to be popular since it opened in 1988, carrying about 30,000 people a day along its 2-mile-long route. Many people who lived in Sydney were concerned that the elevated route would be an eyesore, particularly in older parts of the city. Protesters tried hard to block the monorail's construction. Today, it has become part of everyday life for many people who live in Sydney.

London's LRT

The Docklands Light Railway in London opened in 1987. It was Britain's first Light Rapid Transit (LRT) to have driverless vehicles controlled by a computerized control system. However, it was not Britain's first LRT. That prize went to Newcastle's Tyne and Wear Metro, which began running in 1980. LRTs provide a frequent service, with unstaffed stations and automatic ticket machines. Many cities throughout the world have chosen to install them in preference to monorails because they are cheaper to run.

MONORAIL

MONORAILS DATE back to the 1820s. As with early trains, these early monorails were pulled by horses and carried heavy materials such as building bricks, rather than passengers. About 60 years later, engineers designed steam locomotives that hauled cars along A-shaped frameworks. However, neither the trains nor the cars were very stable. Loads had to be carefully balanced on either side of the A-frame to stop them tipping off.

Today's monorails are completely stable, with several sets of rubber wheels to give a smooth ride. They are powered by electricity, and many are driverless. Like fully automatic LRTs, driverless monorail trains are controlled by computers that tell them when to stop, start, speed up or slow down.

Monorails are not widely used today because they are more expensive to run than two-track railroads. The special monorail track costs more to build and is more of an eyesore than two-track lines. The cars cannot be switched from one track to another, and it is expensive to change or extend a monorail line.

Staying on track
Vertical sets of running wheels carry the weight of this modern monorail and keep it on top of the huge rail. Other horizontal sets of wheels, called guides and stabilizers, run along the sides of the rail. They keep the train on course and stop it from tipping when it goes around bends.

MODEL MONORAIL

You will need: sheet of protective paper, 28¼in length of wood (1½in wide and 1½in deep), acrylic paints, paintbrush, water pot, 26½in length of plastic curtain rail (with screws, end fittings and four plastic runners), saw, screwdriver, sheet of red card, pencil, ruler, scissors, double-sided scotch tape, 7in length of 1in-thick foam board, glue and glue brush, black felt-tip pen.

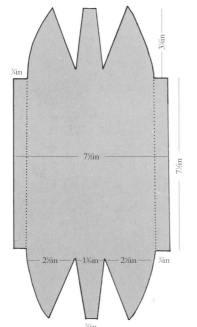

1 Cover the work surface with paper to protect it. Then paint the block of wood yellow. Let the first coat dry thoroughly before applying a second coat of paint.

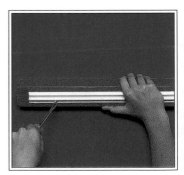

2 Ask an adult to saw the curtain rail to size if necessary. Place the track centrally on the wood and screw it into place. Screw in the end fittings at one end of the rail.

3 Copy the template onto the red card and cut it out. Score along the dotted lines and fold inward. Stick double-sided scotch tape along the outside of each folded section.

4 Remove the backing from the tape. Stick one side of the foam onto it. Fold the card over and press the other piece of double-sided tape to the opposite side of the foam.

5 Overlap the pointed ends at the back and front of the train and glue. Then glue the inside end of the top flaps, back and front. Fold them over and press firmly to secure.

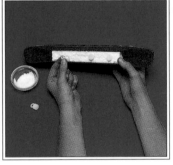

6 Pencil in windows along both sides of the train. Fill them in with a black felt-tip pen. Paint decorative black and yellow stripes along the bottom of the windows.

7 Put a dab of glue on the "eye" end of each plastic runner. Hold the train, foam bottom toward you. Push each runner in turn into the foam at roughly equal intervals.

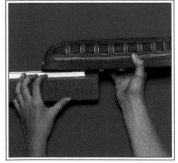

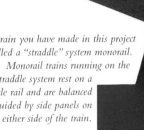

8 Stand the track on a flat surface. At the end of the track without an end stop, feed each plastic runner into the track. Run the train back and forth along the track.

The train you have made in this project is called a "straddle" system monorail. Monorail trains running on the straddle system rest on a single rail and are balanced and guided by side panels on either side of the train.

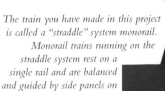

WORKING ON THE RAILROADS

A s the railroads grew ever larger, so did the number of people employed to keep them running safely and on time. In Britain, for example, about 47,000 people worked for the railroad companies by the late 1840s. Today, about 95,000 people are employed on the British railroads—seven times less than during World War I (1914–18). One reason is that some jobs that were once done by people, such as selling tickets, are now done by machines. Automation has not been widespread, however. Most railroads around the world have little money to buy computers and control systems.

Stationmasters and train conductors are just some of the people who talk to passengers and deal with their needs. Most railroad employees work behind the scenes, however, and rarely meet passengers. Managers plan how many trains should run on a particular line, how often, and how fast. Engineering teams check and keep the tracks, signals, and other equipment in safe working order.

Standing on the footplate
Two men worked in the cab. They stood on the footplate because there were no seats. The engineer was in charge. He managed the engine controls and the main brakes and kept a sharp look out for signals and anything blocking the track. The fireman stoked the fire and insured the boiler contained enough water.

Laying track
Track workers check a section of track that has been newly laid with stone ballast, ties, and rail. Rails should be checked regularly for cracks and deterioration. The ground beneath the rail can also subside and twist the rails.

Building trains
Workers in a factory are assembling an aluminum-bodied diesel train. Modern trains are built of either steel or aluminum sections welded together into a strong single unit. Separate units such as the driving cab, air-conditioning engine, and restrooms are fixed on the car later.

In the driving seat

Compared to the older steam engines, life is fairly comfortable in the cabs of modern locomotives. For a start, the engineer can sit down. They are also protected from the weather inside fully enclosed cabs, and they do not have to stick their heads outside to see the track ahead. Today's engineers still manage the controls and brakes, and watch out for signals and obstacles on the track. They also have a lot of help from computerized railroad systems.

Insect debris

The windows of this train are being cleaned by hand, since this is the most effective way to remove the accumulation of flying insects on the cab windows. The bodies of most trains are cleaned in automatic washing plants using revolving brushes, high-pressure water jets, and powerful cleaning agents that meet high environmental standards. In most cases, trains are cleaned every 24 hours when they come back to their home depot for examination and routine servicing.

Chefs on board

Armies of chefs and kitchen staff play an important role in making sure passengers do not go hungry during the journey. Most cooked food is prepared onboard the train using microwave ovens and electric burners. Almost all long-distance trains have dining and lounge cars, where passengers can take refreshments during their journeys. Even smaller trains often have buffet cars or mobile buffet carts.

DRESSED FOR THE JOB

MANY DIFFERENT railroad workers began wearing special hats and uniforms during the 1840s, from train engineers to stationmasters. A uniform makes the wearer look smart and efficient and lets him or her stand out in a crowd. This is essential if a passenger is looking for help in a busy train station. Uniforms are issued by the railroad companies. Each company usually has its own special design for hat badges and uniform buttons.

In the past, different kinds of hat or badge often went with different jobs. The engineers of steam locomotives, for example, used to wear caps with shiny tops. Firemen were not issued with hats or uniforms. They wore overalls and often covered their heads with a knotted handkerchief. The first stationmasters wore top hats instead of caps to show how important they were. When they later switched to caps, the brim was often decorated with gold braid, similar to the one you can make in this project.

Dressed for the job
A stationmaster and conductor at Osaka Railway Station in Japan wear their distinctive dark uniforms, caps, and sashes. The stationmaster, or area manager, has an extremely important role in running the railroads. He or she is in charge of all aspects of running the station and must insure that trains arrive and depart on time.

STATIONMASTER'S CAP

You will need: *thin red card measuring 24 x 3½in, masking tape, thin red card measuring 4¼ x 4¼in, pencil, scissors, thin red card measuring 10¼ x 6in, glue and glue brush, sheet of white paper, pair of compasses, black felt, black paint, paintbrush, water pot, 16in length of gold braid, extra card, gold paint.*

1 Wrap the 24 x 3½in piece of red card around your head to get the right size. Then stick the two ends together with masking tape to make the circular crown of the hat.

2 Place the crown on the 4½ x 4½in piece of red card. Hold the crown firmly and draw around it on to the flat piece of card. Cut out the circle to make the top of your hat.

3 Place the card circle on top of the crown of the hat. Join the two parts of the hat together using lots of strips of masking tape all the way around the join.

4 Place the hat over part of the 10¼ x 6in piece of card. Draw a semicircle by tracing around the hat edge. Start from one end of the semicircle, and draw a crescent shape as shown.

5 Use a pair of compasses to draw another semicircle ⅜in in from the first. Cut out the crescent shape. Make cuts into the inner semicircle band all the way around to make tabs.

6 Fold the tabs up and glue around the edge of the crown where the peak will go. Fit the tabs inside the crown and stick them down. Cover the tabs with tape to hold firm.

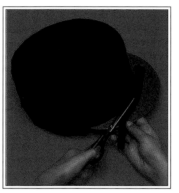

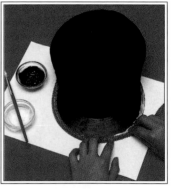

7 Place the hat, top down, onto a sheet of paper. Draw and cut out a circle ½in wider than the hat. Pin it on the felt and cut out a felt circle. Glue this on to the top of the hat.

8 Cut a 24 x 4in piece of felt. Glue this to the side of the hat, folding under at the bottom. At the peak, make a ⅜in cut in the felt, and trim off the excess as shown.

9 Give the peak two coats of black paint. Let the paint dry between coats. Then glue on a piece of gold braid as shown above.

10 Design your own hat badge or copy the one shown in the picture. Draw it on a small piece of card and paint it gold. When the paint is dry, cut it out. Glue it to the front of the hat.

If you have a whistle, you could attach it to a piece of gold ribbon and hang it around your neck to complete the outfit.

TRAVELING IN STYLE

IT WAS some time before traveling on a passenger train was as comfortable as waiting in one of the splendid stations. Before the 1850s, there were few luxuries and no restrooms, even on long journeys. The overall comfort of the journey depended on how much money you had paid for your ticket. First-class cars were—and still are—the most expensive and the most comfortable way to travel. Then came second class, third class, and sometimes even fourth class.

The pioneer of comfortable rail travel was a US businessman called George Pullman. In 1859, after a particularly unpleasant train journey, he designed a coach in which "people could sleep and eat with more ease and comfort." Pullman launched his sleeping car in 1864, and was soon exporting luxury sleeping and dining cars around the world.

First-class comforts
By the late 1800s, first-class passengers such as these elegantly dressed ladies enjoyed every comfort on their journey. There were soft, padded benches and armchairs and cloth-covered tea tables. The design of luxury railroad cars was based on that of top-class hotels. Windows had thick, plush curtains and fittings were made of polished wood and shiny brass.

Royal seal of approval
This luxurious railroad car was made specially for Britain's Queen Victoria, who reigned from 1837 until her death in 1901. It had padded walls, thick carpets, expensive paintings on the walls, and the finest decoration. Many European kings and queens had their own cars built so that they could travel in royal style. Queen Victoria's royal car included a sleeping compartment, and it is thought she enjoyed sleeping in it more than at her palaces.

The Blue Train
South Africa's Blue Trains run between Cape Town and Pretoria in South Africa and are regarded as the most luxurious trains in the world. Passengers benefit from a 24-hour butler and laundry service and two lounge cars, and all the suites are equipped with televisions and telephones.

Lap of luxury

The *Orient-Express* first graced the railroads of Europe in 1883. It formed a scheduled link between Paris, France, and Bucharest in Romania. The scheduled service stopped running in May 1977, and it was replaced by a new "tourist-only" *Orient-Express* in May 1982. Passengers can once again enjoy the comfortable sleeping cars with velvet curtains, plush seats, and five-course French cuisine in a Pullman dining car like the one shown above.

A rocky ride

The Canadian has a domed glass roof so that it offers spectacular views during the 2,776-mile journey from Toronto, on the east coast of Canada, to Vancouver, on the west. The journey lasts for three days and takes in the rolling prairies of Saskatchewan, Edmonton, and Alberta. It then begins the gradual ascent through the foothills of the Rocky Mountains.

Lounging about

Long-distance trains on the Indian Pacific line from Sydney, on the Pacific Ocean, to Perth, on the Indian Ocean, are well equipped for the 65-hour journey across Australia. Indeed, they are described as being "luxury hotels on wheels." Passengers can relax and enjoy the entertainment provided in the comfortable surroundings of the train's lounge cars. These trains also have cafeterias, smart dining cars, club cars, and two classes of accommodation. Passengers can eat, drink, and sleep in comfort. The trains are even equipped with a honeymoon suite and a sick bay.

ADVERTISING

IN THE early days of the railroads, radio and television had not been invented. Rail companies had to rely on printed advertisements to attract passengers. Posters have long been used to attract train travelers. At first, they were little more than printed handbills—a few words with the odd black-and-white picture. "The Wonder of 1851! From York to London and back for a Crown," read one British rail-company poster. A crown was 5 shillings (the equivalent of 35¢ in today's money).

Early posters were so basic because machines for printing words and color pictures were not developed until the late 1800s. Posters soon became more colorful. For example, the French railroads used eye-catching posters to advertise their new electric services in the early 1900s. The pictures on early railroad posters usually showed the destination rather than the train—people travel on trains because they want to go somewhere, after all. By promoting new services and encouraging people to take the train on vacation and on one-day trips, rail companies helped to improve advertising methods.

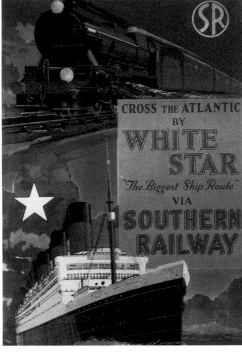

Atlantic crossing
Britain's Southern Railway promoted both its own train services and those of shipping company White Star in this poster from the late 1920s. Passengers could take the train to Southampton in England and then join a White Star ship for the crossing to New York in the USA. At that time, many railroads owned shipping lines or worked with steamship companies.

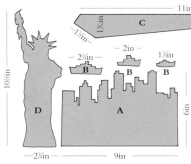

MAKE A POSTER

You will need: *protective paper, dark blue card (10½ x 9in), acrylic paints, paintbrush, water pot, glue and glue brush, cream card (14¼ x 10in), light blue card (9 x 3⅛ and 12 x 2in), pencil, ruler, scissors, large sheet of black card, blue card (9 x 2¼in), yellow card (12 x 4in), black pen.*

1 Cover the work surface and lay the dark blue card on to it. Mix some yellow and white paint, load a paintbrush with paint and then flick spots on to the card as shown above.

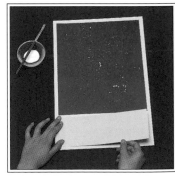

2 Glue the dark blue card onto the cream card, leaving a ⅛in border at top and sides and 3¾in at the bottom. Glue the 9 x 3⅛in light blue card at the bottom as shown.

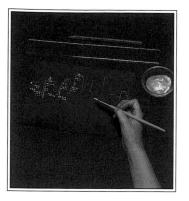

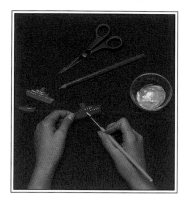

3 Copy the New York skyline template (A) using the black card. Use the yellow-and-white paint mixture to make spots for lights in the windows. Cut the skyline out.

4 When the paint is completely dry, glue the back of the skyline template. Line up the bottom edge with the top edge of the light blue card and then press down firmly.

5 Copy and cut out the ship templates (B) using the black card. Use the yellow-and-white paint mixture to paint portholes on the ships. Leave the paint to dry.

7 Copy the statue template (D) or enlarge it on a photocopier and trace it on to yellow card. Add details with black felt tip pen. Cut out the statue and glue it in position.

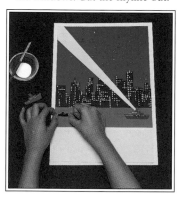

6 Glue the blue card on to the bottom of the skyline. Then glue on the ships. Copy and cut out the spotlight template (C) using the 30 x 5cm light blue card and glue on the largest ship as shown above.

NEW YORK
BY TRAIN

Now that you know how to make a poster, you can design your own. Collect photographs and cuttings from magazines and tourist information leaflets of a town or a famous tourist attraction nearby. Photocopy them to the size you want and then trace them on to card in the same way you have done for this project.

TRAINS ON FILM

WHEN THE French brothers Auguste and Louis Lumière showed one of their short films in 1895 of a train pulling into a station, many of the audience fled. They were terrified that the train would burst out of the screen into the room. Hardly anyone had ever seen a moving picture before, and people found them frighteningly realistic.

Trains have had a starring role in the movies ever since. The climax of many early movies, for example, involved the "baddies" tying the heroine to a railway track, while the hero rushed to save her. Filmmakers have continued to use trains to keep audiences on the edge of their seats. Nearly all the best train movies have been adventure thrillers.

In the early days, filming moving trains was a risky business. The cameras were bolted on the locomotive, while the camera operator leaned out or rode on a train on a parallel track. Such risks in filming would not be taken today.

Poetry, please
Night Mail (1936) showed scenes of mail being dropped off, and collected, by the "Night Mail" train in Scotland. It was made to show how letters were carried on the mail train between England and Scotland. Later, the British-born American poet W. H. Auden was asked to write verse for a voice-over. His poetry echoes the noises of the train as it made its long journey through the night.

Tears on the train
In the 1945 movie *Brief Encounter*, two people (actors Trevor Howard and Celia Johnson) find romance in a railroad station. Their love is doomed, however, as both are married. Much of the action was shot at Carnforth Station in Britain.

Railway children to the rescue
When a landslide threatens to derail a steam train in *The Railway Children* (1970), the children save the day by turning red petticoats into a warning signal for the engineer. The movie used old engines and coaches on a heritage railway in Yorkshire, Britain. It gives an insight into how steam trains and local stations operated in the early 1900s.

Smashing finish

A runaway train crashes through the walls of the station concourse in the thrilling climax to the 1976 action movie *Silver Streak*. Almost the whole movie is set on the train, during its two-and-a-half-day journey from Los Angeles to Chicago in the USA. Gene Wilder stars as the passenger who witnesses a murder on his first night and spends the rest of the journey battling off the baddies.

Bond on board

Roger Moore plays the smooth British agent in the 13th James Bond movie, *Octopussy* (released in 1983). Like all Bond movies, it is packed with breathtaking stunts and chases. During a gripping sequence onboard a speeding train, Bond survives crawling below, along the sides, and over the roof of the cars. He also manages to jump off the train without getting hurt. Not something the rest of us should try! Sequences for the movie were shot on real trains moving at low speeds. Stunt men were used for the most dangerous scenes.

Animal mischief

Indiana Jones and the Last Crusade (released in 1989) opens with a thrilling flashback. Young Indie is trying to escape pursuers by clambering along the top of a steam train. Chases are the stock-in-trade of adventure movies, but this one is different. The steam locomotive is hauling circus cars. Indie falls into various cages, where he finds snakes, a rhinoceros, and even a lion!

Race to the death

A speeding freight train carrying a stolen nuclear weapon is the setting for the nail-biting closing sequence of the 1996 action movie *Broken Arrow*. The hero (shown left, played by Christian Slater) scrambles over and under the freight cars as he attempts to wrest control of the train back from the villain (played by John Travolta) and disarm the bomb before it explodes.

RECORD BREAKERS

BIGGEST, FASTEST, steepest—trains and railroads have been setting records ever since they were invented. Official speed records began when George and Robert Stephenson's *Rocket* reached a top speed of 30mph in the 1829 Rainhill Trials. By the end of the 1800s, engineers were competing to produce a steam engine that could break the 100mph speed record.

Timekeeping was inaccurate until speedometers were fitted to locomotives during the 1900s. An American *No. 999* locomotive may have briefly managed 100mph in 1893. The first steam trains capable of sustaining this kind of speed over long distances did not enter service until the 1930s.

World records are usually set over short distances, by locomotives hauling fewer carriages. When, for example, the 200mph-barrier was broken in 1955 by two French Railways electric locomotives, each one was hauling just three cars.

Claim to fame
The New York Central & Hudson River Railroad (NYC & HRR) built the 4-4-0 *No. 999* to haul its Empire State Express. On May 11, 1893, it was claimed that *No. 999* recorded a run of 112mph between New York and Buffalo. The V-shaped "plow" at the front was one of the distinctive features of American locomotives. Since great lengths of the American railroads were not fenced off, it was essential to protect the front of the locomotives from wandering animals such as buffaloes. The plow performed this function very well.

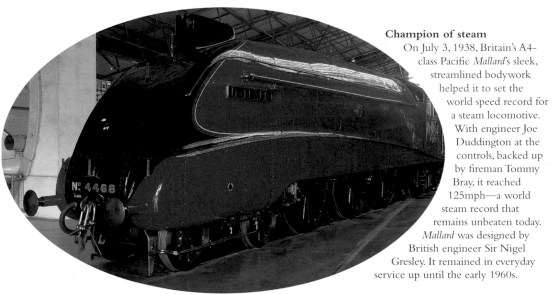

Champion of steam
On July 3, 1938, Britain's A4-class Pacific *Mallard*'s sleek, streamlined bodywork helped it to set the world speed record for a steam locomotive. With engineer Joe Duddington at the controls, backed up by fireman Tommy Bray, it reached 125mph—a world steam record that remains unbeaten today. *Mallard* was designed by British engineer Sir Nigel Gresley. It remained in everyday service up until the early 1960s.

Steep slopes

The *Pilatusbahn* in Lucerne, Switzerland, is the steepest incline (rack-and-pinion) railroad in the world, climbing to a height of 6,791ft above sea level. This system uses a rack laid between the rails. This links with a cog wheel under the engine as it drives the train up the steep 1:2 gradients (1 yard up for every 2 yards along).

Overcoming the obstacles

Mount Washington Railway in New Hampshire in the USA became the world's first mountain incline railroad when it opened in 1869. At this time, mountain climbing and sightseeing by steam railroad were great tourist attractions.

Shapes and sizes

1. Scotsman Patrick Stirling's Single locomotives, dating from 1870, are particularly striking locomotives. The driving wheels of these steam engines were a massive 8ft in diameter.
2. The fastest electric trains are the French TGV (*Train à Grande Vitesse*). A modified TGV unit set the current world speed record of 320mph.
3. By winning the Rainhill Trials in 1829, Robert and George Stephenson's *Rocket* put steam travel firmly on the world map, making this one of the most famous steam locomotives in the world.
4. The world's largest and most powerful steam engines are undoubtedly the Union Pacific Big Boys, each weighing over 550 tons.

1
13½ft
52½ft

2
13½ft
72ft

3
16ft
24ft

4
16ft
132½ft

HIGH–SPEED TRAINS

THE RECORD-HOLDERS of today are the high-speed electric trains that whisk passengers between major city centers at 155–185mph. These high-speed trains are the railroad's answer to the competition from airplanes and freeways that grew up after World War II (1939–45). High-speed trains can travel at well over the legal limits for road traffic. Although they cannot travel as fast as planes, they save passengers time by taking them to city centers. In some cases, high-speed trains even beat the flying time between major cities such as London and Paris.

The world's first high-speed intercity passenger service was launched in Japan on October 1, 1964. It linked the capital, Tokyo, with the major industrial city of Osaka in the south. The average speed of these trains—137mph—broke all the records for a passenger train service. The service was officially named the *Tokaido Shinkansen* (new high-speed railroad), but the trains soon became known as Bullet Trains to describe their speed and the bullet-shaped noses of the locomotives.

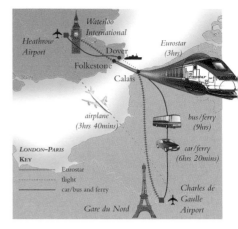

Market leader
The Eurostar has become the quickest way to travel between the city centers London, Britain, and Paris, France. It cuts out time-consuming airport check-in and transfer periods. Ferry crossings dramatically increase the journey times by car and by bus.

Rocket on rails
The latest high-speed JR500 trains to operate on Japan's *Tokaido Shinkansen* are as streamlined as a jet plane. Today, they can haul their 16 passenger carriages at 185mph. The average speed of the trains in 1960 was 135mph.

Stacking the odds

On some high-speed trains, such as this French TGV, passengers ride in double-decker cars. The initials "TGV" are short for *Train à Grande Vitesse* (high-speed train). The operational speed of these French trains is 185mph. TGVs also hold the current world speed record for a wheeled train. On May 18, 1990, a TGV Atlantique reached an amazing 320mph.

Swedish tilter

The Swedish X2000 tilting electric trains have an average speed of 95mph and a top speed of 125mph. Tilting trains lean into curves to allow them to travel around bends at faster speeds than non-tilting trains.

Melting the ICE

Germany's ICE (InterCity Express) high-speed trains reached speeds of more than 250mph during tests, before they entered service in 1992. Their maximum operating speed is about 175mph. Like other high-speed trains, they are streamlined to reduce the slowing effects of drag.

Spanish speeders

Spain's elegant high-speed trains are called AVEs (*Alta Velocidad España,* or high speed of Spain). Their average operational speed is about 135mph. They entered service on Spain's first high-speed railroad, between Madrid and Seville, in 1992. The AVEs' design was based on the French TGVs. AVEs are made in France with some Spanish parts. Like all high-speed trains, AVEs take their power from overhead electricity lines.

INVESTING IN THE FUTURE

To ACCELERATE to speeds of up to 185–215mph, trains need to run on specially constructed tracks, with as few curves and slopes as possible. The tracks have to be wider apart than was usual in the past. A speeding train stirs the wind into eddies, which can buffet a passing train and jolt its passengers. The ride is also smoother and faster if continuously welded rails are used. If they have their own, dedicated lines, high-speed trains do not have to fit in with the timetables of ordinary, less speedy trains that would slow them down.

Star performers
The Eurostar trains operate between England and Continental Europe. They can accelerate to 185mph only when they reach the specially built, high-speed railroad lines in France. The speed of the trains through southern England is limited because they run on normal track. Work on a new, British, high-speed line, the Channel Tunnel Rail Link between London St. Pancras and Folkestone, is underway. It is expected to be completed in 2007 at a cost of more than $8 billion.

Throughout the world, railroad companies are investing billions of dollars in building new lines or upgrading old track to carry their high-speed trains. In a few countries, people believe the future of land travel lies with an entirely different kind of train. Called maglevs, these trains "fly" less than an inch above the track, raised and propelled by magnetism.

Scandinavian shuttle
These sleek, three-car, stainless-steel electric trains began running late in 1999 on a new railroad built to link the center of Oslo, the capital of Norway, with the new Gardermoen Airport, 30 miles to the north of the city. The maximum speed of these trains is 130mph, which enables them to cover the journey in just over 19 minutes. The line includes Norway's longest railroad tunnel at just under 8½ miles.

Virgin express
Britain's Virgin Trains is investing a lot of money in new high-speed electric trains for its West Coast route between London and Glasgow. Work on upgrading old track to carry the trains is also underway. If all goes to plan, journey times between the two cities will be reduced from just over five hours in 1999 to just under four hours in 2005.

High-speed magnetism

Japanese maglev (short for magnetic levitation) trains have reached the astonishing speed of 343mph on this specially constructed Yamanashi test line. This outstrips the world's fastest wheeled train, the TGV, by 24mph. Maglevs are so speedy because they float above their track. They do not have wheels and they do not touch the rails. Rails solved the problem of the slowing force of friction between wheels and roads. Maglevs are the answer to reducing friction between wheels and rails.

Spanish AVE
Based on the design of the French TGV, the average operational speed of these trains is around 135mph.

French TGV
A slightly modified TGV unit set the current world speed record for a train in a trial in 1990, reaching 320mph.

British Pendolino
A new generation of British high-speed tilting trains, designed to reach speeds of 135mph.

German ICE
A former world speed record holder in 1988, reaching 250mph. These trains entered into service in 1991.

Italian Pendolino
These trains run at speeds of around 155mph on the existing network in Italy, tilting as they travel around curves.

------- High-speed lines—existing or under construction
------- Planned high-speed lines

On the move in Europe

Many European railroads are planning to develop high-speed rail networks over the next few years. One of the fastest routes will be the high-speed link between Madrid and Barcelona in Spain. The line will have some of the world's fastest passenger trains in service, running at speeds of up to 215mph. By 2007, Spain will have 4,500 miles of high-speed rail networks with a fleet of over 280 trains.

By 2004 in France, tilting trains will cut around 30 minutes off the journey time between Paris and Toulouse. Some of the fastest short-distance trains are running in Norway between Oslo and Gardermoen Airport. They travel at up to 130mph and cover 30 miles in just 19 minutes.

FLOATING TRAINS

Maglev (magnetically levitated) trains need their own specially constructed tracks, called guideways, to move along. The trains are raised and propelled by powerful electromagnets. The special thing about magnets is that "unlike" poles (north and south) attract each other or pull together, while "like" poles (north and north, or south and south) repel or push apart. To make an electromagnet, an electric current flows through a wire or other conductor. When the direction of the current is changed, the magnetic poles switch, too.

A maglev train rises when one set of electromagnets beneath it repels another set in the guideway. The maglev is propelled by other electromagnets changing magnetic fields (switching poles). A set of electromagnets in the guideway ahead attracts electromagnets beneath the train, pulling it forward. As the train passes, the electromagnetic fields are switched. The maglev is repelled and pushed onward to the next set of magnets on the guideway.

The main advantage of maglevs over normal wheeled trains is that they are faster because they are not slowed by friction. In tests in Germany in 1993, a maglev train reached speeds of 280mph. Maglevs are also quieter and use less energy than wheeled trains.

Maglevs get moving
The technology behind maglevs was developed in the 1960s. The world's first service opened at Birmingham City Airport in Britain in the mid-1980s. Japan and Germany now lead the field in developing the technology. When the German Transrapid maglevs start running between Berlin and Hamburg in 2005, they will provide the world's first high-speed intercity maglev service.

MODEL MAGLEV

You will need: yellow card, pencil, ruler, scissors, red card, green card, glue and glue brush, blue card, double-sided scotch tape, 12 x 4in wooden board, bradawl, two 3¼in lengths thin dowel, wood glue, green and red paint, paintbrush, water pot, four magnets with holes drilled in their centers.

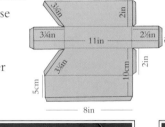

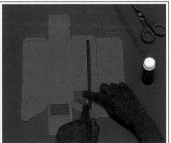

1 Copy the template on to a thin piece of yellow card. The tabs around the side of the template should be ½in wide. Carefully cut around the outline.

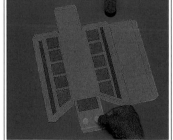

2 Cut two strips of red card and glue them to each side of the template as shown. Cut the green card into window shapes and glue them to the front and sides.

3 Continue to glue the windows to each side of the train to make two even rows. Cut two small blue card circles for headlights. Glue them to the front of the train as shown.

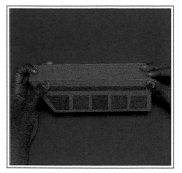

4 Leave the train template until the glue is completely dry. Then carefully use a pair of scissors and a ruler to score along the dotted lines for the tabs and the folds of the train.

5 Bend along the scored lines to form the basic shape of the train as shown above. Then cut small strips of double-sided scotch tape and stick them along each tab.

6 Stick the front and back sections of the train to the tabs on one side of the train. Repeat for the other side. Then stick the base section of the train to the opposite side.

7 Use a bradawl to pierce two holes in the wooden base, 3½in in from each end. Enlarge with a pencil. Put wood glue on the end of each piece of dowel and push one into each hole.

8 When the glue is dry give the base a coat of green paint. Paint two coats, letting the first dry before you apply the second. Then paint the dowel uprights a bright red.

9 Press the two magnets together so that they repel. These sides are the same poles—north or south. Use double-sided tape to fix the magnets to the base with like poles facing up.

Push the train over the dowel uprights. Like poles on the wooden base and the train base face each other, making the train "float" in midair. You can feel the magnetic force if you push down on the top of the train.

10 Hold the base of the train up to the dowel uprights. Mark two points in the center of the base the same distance as between the uprights. Pierce through the marks.

11 Push magnets over the dowel uprights to repel those on the base. Take them off and tape them over the holes in the train base so that these like poles face upward.

GLOSSARY

Alta Velocidad Españã (AVE)
The name of the high-speed passenger trains that operate in Spain.

Automatic Train Protection (ATP)
An advanced safety system operating on some trains running on British railroad networks. Trains pick up electronic signals from the track, which tell the engineer to slow or stop the train. ATP automatically slows the train if the engineer exceeds the speed limit.

Automatic Warning System (AWS)
A safety feature of all trains operating on British railroad networks. AWS tells the engineer whether the track ahead is clear. Electric magnets between the rails send a message to the train, causing a bell to sound in the engineer's cab if the track is clear. Otherwise, the magnet stays "dead" and a horn sounds. AWS operates the brakes automatically if the engineer does not respond to the signals.

boiler
The part of a steam engine where steam is produced through the action of heat on water in the boiler tubes.

buffer
Rigid metal structures that absorb the impact of a train to stop it at the end of the track.

Bullet Train
The name of the high-speed, streamlined passenger trains that operate in Japan.

caboose
A vehicle at the back of trains. A brakeman riding in the caboose applies brakes in the caboose on instruction from the engineer in the locomotive. This insured that all the cars of the train stayed coupled.

car
An individual compartment of a train that carries the passengers. A car is also known as a coach.

catenary
An overhead power cable supplying electricity to a train through a pantograph attached to the top of the locomotive.

conductor
The person responsible for the safety of passengers on a train. The conductor checks, and sometimes issues, tickets for passengers on the train.

container
An enormous metal box that carries freight during its transportation. Containers make it easy to combine different methods of transportation, such as sea and rail, in one journey.

coupler
A connecting device that joins a locomotive to a car or freight car to make a train.

coupling rod
A link that connects the driving wheels on both sides of a locomotive. Coupling rods stop the wheels from slipping and even out the power distributed by the steam engine.

cut-and-cover construction
An early method of building underground tunnels. A large trench is cut into the earth along the line of the tunnel, the tunnel is lined with bricks, and then the tunnel is roofed over. Cut-and-cover construction has been eclipsed by the development of powerful digging devices called Tunnel-Boring Machines (TBMs).

cylinder
An enclosed part of a steam engine that houses the moving piston.

driving wheel
The wheel of a locomotive that turns in response to power from the cylinder.

flange
A rim on the inside of the metal wheel of a locomotive that stops the wheels slipping sideways and falling off the rails.

freight
Goods transported by rail, road, sea, or air.

friction
A force that stops or slows an object moving while it is in contact with another object. Friction results when a train wheel moves over a rail.

funicular
A railroad that hauls one car up and one car down steep slopes. Cars move up and down the slope as a cable attached to each car winds around an electrically powered drum.

gauge
The width between the inside edges of the rails of a railroad track. In Britain, the United States, and most of Europe, the gauge is 4ft 8½in.

humpyard
An area next to a main railroad route where freight cars can be sorted to make freight trains. The freight cars are pushed uphill over a hump in the yard, and travel by gravity into sidings on the other side.

incline (rack-and-pinion) railroad
A railroad that operates on steep slopes. A cogwheel underneath the passenger car engages in teeth on a central rail that runs up the slope.

InterCity Express (ICE)
The name of the high-speed passenger trains that operate in Germany.

leading truck
The pair of wheels at the front of a locomotive.

locomotive
A detachable, wheeled engine used to pull the cars of a train. Steam and diesel engines generate their own power. Electric locomotives collect electricity from an external source.

maglev train
A high-speed, streamlined train that is raised above a track called a guideway and moves through the action of powerful electromagnets.

monorail
A train that runs on a single rail.

pantograph
An triangular assembly atop of an electric locomotive that draws electricity from an overhead power cable called a catenary. This electricity is then used to move the train.

pendolino
A train that tilts from side to side, enabling the train to move around curves at higher speeds than non-tilting trains.

piston
A device that moves backward and forward within the cylinder of a steam engine. Each piston transforms steam pressure into the movement of the wheels of the locomotive.

plow
A sloping V-shaped plate or grid attached to the front of American locomotives. The plow is designed to clear cattle and other obstructions from the line.

Pullman
A car where passengers can eat and sleep in luxurious surroundings.

railcar
A self-propelled passenger vehicle powered by diesel or electricity.

rolling stock
The locomotives, cars, and any other vehicles that operate on a railroad.

safety valves
Valves set to lift automatically to allow steam to escape if the boiler pressure exceeds a safe limit.

signals
Messages transmitted to the cab of a locomotive to tell the engineer if the track ahead is clear of other locomotives. When the railroads first started in the mid-1800s, railroad policemen standing at the side of the track signaled to engineers with their hands. Today, electronic signals are transmitted directly to the tower.

smokebox
The front section of a steam locomotive boiler where the exhaust collects before escaping through the smokestack.

straddle system
Monorails running on the straddle system rest on a single rail and are balanced and guided by side panels on either side of the train.

switches
Rails on the track that guide the wheels of a locomotive onto a different section of track.

tie
A horizontal concrete beam that supports the rails on a railroad track.

train
A number of passenger or freight cars coupled together. Trains can be self-propelled or hauled by a locomotive.

***Train à Grande Vitesse* (TGV)**
The name of the high-speed, streamlined passenger trains that operate in France.

Train Protection and Warning System (TPWS)
An improved version of the British safety feature AWS. TPWS uses AWS safety measures but also incorporates an automatic stop at a red signal and a speed trap in advance of the signal.

truck
A unit placed underneath a locomotive that guides the train around curves in the track. The truck also provides extra support for the locomotive. Four or six pivoted wheels are mounted on one truck.

INDEX